The Kingdom and the Garden

The Kingdom and the Garden

GIORGIO AGAMBEN

TRANSLATED BY ADAM KOTSKO

LONDON NEW YORK CALCUTTA

SERIES EDITOR
Alberto Toscano

Seagull Books, 2024

Originally published in Italian as *Il regno e il giardino*
© 2019 Neri Pozza Editore, Vicenza

First published in English translation by Seagull Books, 2020
English translation © Adam Kotsko, 2020

ISBN 978 1 80309 364 2

British Library Cataloguing-in-Publication Data
A catalogue record for this book is available from the British Library

Typeset by Seagull Books, Calcutta, India
Printed and bound by WordsWorth India, New Delhi, India

❀

Contents

1

The Garden of Earthly Delights

1.1. In 1947, Wilhelm Fraenger, a German scholar who was part of the group of intellectuals who assembled around the Dutch journal *Castrum Peregrini*, published a new interpretation of Hieronymus Bosch's triptych in the Museo del Prado, known as *The Garden of Earthly Delights*. According to Fraenger, the meaning of the enigmatic triptych is clarified only if we return it to the theological context from which it arose: the heresy of the Free Spirit or of the *homines intelligentiae*, to which Jacob van Almaengien, who commissioned and inspired it, belonged. The brothers of the Free Spirit professed that spiritual perfection coincided with the advent of the Kingdom and the restoration of the Edenic innocence which humanity had enjoyed in the earthly paradise. Concluding his meticulous interpretation of the triptych's figures, Fraenger writes:

> The kingdom of the Spirit has been restored; the *evangelium aeternum* has become flesh and blood in countless awakened human beings who are already living in a state of paradisical innocence on earth. [. . .] The disciples of the Free Spirit were accustomed to call their devotional community life 'Paradise' and interpreted the word as signifying the 'quintessence of love'. It is in this sense that the 'Paradise' of the central panel must be understood. What it shows is an idealized reality, a 'today' at once real and mystery, symbolic down to its most minute details. This instantaneity determines the whole composition of the triptych. Instead of the representation of a chronological sequence, in which the Garden of Eden—the beginning of all things—would have been separated from the 'Paradise' of the central panel—the future restoration of the original condition—we find here the perfect simultaneity of a single state of consciousness (Fränger 1951: 103–04).

It is not surprising, therefore, that Fraenger, precisely at the beginning of his investigation, discretely substitutes for the traditional title—*The Garden of Earthly Delights*—the unheard-of rubric 'The Millennial Kingdom' (*das tausend-jährige Reich*): '*The Millennial Kingdom*, at Madrid, generally known as *The Garden of Earthly Delights* [. . .]' (ibid.: 2). That a title that refers to a political-theological theme—the Kingdom—should be closely associated in this way with Adam's dwelling place in the earthly paradise is nevertheless not something to be taken for granted.

It is of this theological paradigm—the Garden of Eden which, while it appears from the very beginning in an eminent position in theological reflection, has been tenaciously displaced to the margins of the tradition of Western thought—that the present study proposes to trace a brief genealogy. While the Kingdom, with its economic-trinitarian counterpart, has indeed never ceased to influence the forms and structures of profane power, the Garden, despite its constitutive political vocation (it was 'planted' in Eden for the happy habitation of humanity), has remained substantially alien to it. Even when, as has happened many times, groups of people have sought to draw from it the inspiration for a model of decisively het-erodox community, the dominant strategy has always been vigilant to neutralize its political implications. And yet, as Fraenger's hypothesis suggests, not only is it not possible to separate the Garden from the Kingdom, but they are on the contrary so frequently and so intimately intertwined that it is likely that precisely a study of their intersections and their divergences would wind up reshaping to a significant extent the cartography of Western power.

1.2. The history of the word 'paradise', which sounds so familiar to us, is a succession of loans from one language to another, as if the foreign term were for some reason always held to be untranslatable or else one wanted at every cost to avoid its obvious equivalent. The Greek term *paradeisos*, which Latin transcribes as *paradisus* and which appears for the first time in Xenophon, is in fact, according to the lexicons, a calque of the Avestic *pairidaeza*, which designates a spacious walled garden (*pairi* means 'around' and *daeza* 'wall'). It is possible that, in recalquing the Iranian term instead of using the Greek word for 'garden', *kēpos*, Xenophon—as specialists still do today, when they leave untranslated exotic terms from the foreign language in which they are experts—meant to show off his knowledge of Persian affairs, which he seems to have cared a great deal about. It is certain, in any case, that he could not imagine that his Greek-Iranian neologism was destined to furnish to Christian theology one of its essential technical terms and to the imagination of the West one of its most persistent fantasies. In that sort of ethnographic novel that is the *Cyropaedia*, he calls *paradeisos* the garden in which Astyages, the grandfather of Cyrus, hunted wild animals. Having become king, Cyrus ordered his satraps to plant some *paradeisoi*, so that the nobles of his retinue, by going hunting, may train in combat, 'for he considered hunting the best preparation for war [. . .] and every time he was constrained to remain in his palace, he would hunt the animals that were in his *paradeisos*' (*Cyropaedia* 7.1.34–8). Even if we should not forget that, in its first appearance in the Greek language, paradise has to do with hunting and war, it is rather in the *Oeconomicus*, a work that had wide diffusion in Greek culture, that Xenophon describes a *paradeisos* more similar to what would become the Western paradigm of the Garden. As it is related by the Spartan Lysander, Cyrus the Younger had shown him his *paradeisos* in Sardis in which the trees were planted at uniform distances in perfectly straight lines, with such geometrical harmony and such 'variety and sweetness of scents that accompanied them as they walked' that Lysander had exclaimed: 'I admire you, Cyrus, for so much beauty, but I admire even more the one who planned and arranged all this.' 'I planned and arranged all these trees,' Cyrus responded to him, 'and many of them I planted myself (*ephyteusa autos*)' (*Oeconomicus* 4.20–23).

1.3. The event that is decisive in every sense for the history of the term was the choice of the Septuagint to translate with *paradeisos* the Hebrew *gan* in Genesis 2:8 (and eight other times in the following verses): *Kai ephyteusen kyrios ho theos paradeison en Edem* ('And God planted a paradise in Eden'). The attempts to justify this choice (for example, by associating, as Jan N. Bremmer does with absolute arbitrarity, the expression *paradeisos tēs tryphēs*, 'garden of delight', in Genesis 3:23 with the names Tryphon and Tryphaena, from monarchs and princesses of Ptolemaic Egypt [Bremmer 2008: 53–4]) are completely inconsistent. One can only ascertain that, when they had to translate the Hebrew *gan*, they preferred to substitute for the common *kēpos* a word that was rarer, genealogically associated with an idea of royalty and prestige and with the presence of animals and water, which was better suited to a garden planted by God.

In any case, an examination of the occurrences of the term in the Septuagint outside of Genesis shows that it has a technical significance and always refers more or less explicitly to the 'garden of God'. The relation is clear in Ezekiel 28:13: 'a crown of beauty in the delight of the garden of God (*en tē tryphē tou paradeisou tou theou*)', and 31:9: 'all the trees of the garden of delight of God (*tou paradeisou tēs tryphēs tou theou*)'. Thus in Joel 2:3: 'as the garden of delight is the land before you', and in Numbers 24:6, in which paradise is associated (as in Genesis 2:10–14: from Eden there springs a river that divides into four branches, Pishon, Gihon, Tigris and Euphrates) with rivers: 'like shaded woods and like gardens beside a river (*osei paradeisoi epi potamoi*)'. Particularly significant are two passages in which *paradeisos* is juxtaposed promiscuously to *kēpos*: in the first (Isaiah 1:29–30: 'They will be ashamed of their gardens [*epi tois kēpois autōn*] which they have desired and the trees will be like terebinths thrown away and like a garden without water [*hōs paradeisos hydor mē echōn*]'), *kēpos* is a generic garden, which can also be deprived of water, while the *paradeisos*, the garden of God, by definition cannot be. No less instructive is the second passage, the famous invocation of Song of Songs 4:12–13: 'You are an enclosed garden (*kēpos kekleismenos*), sister and spouse, an enclosed garden. [. . .] your buds a garden of rivers (*paradeisos roōn*) with fruits of tall trees.' To the indelible image of the *horus conclusus* there is counterposed that of the paradise of delight, whose fruits are not only 'beautiful to see' (*ōraion eis orasis*) but also 'good to eat' (*kalon eis brōsin*) (Genesis 2:9).

1.4. No less significant is the gesture in which, apparently with no hesitation, Jerome decides to translate the term *Eden* from the Hebrew text with *voluptas*: *plantavit autem paradisum voluptatis a principio*, 'God planted in the beginning a garden of delight.'

Eden deliciae interpretatur, he hastily writes in his *Annotations to Genesis*, putting forward as the sole argument for his choice Symmachus' version in Greek, which is not even pertinent: *pro quo Symmacus transtulit paradisum florentem* ('Eden means delight, for which reason Symmachus translates paradise as flower') (Jerome 1959: 4). The nonchalance with which he alters the text of the *Vetus latina* (*Et plantavit Deus paradisum in Eden ad orientem*) is even more surprising in so far as, in the same passage, he takes care to justify his translation *a principio*, instead of *ad orientem*, by invoking the example of Aquila, Symmachus and Theodotion, and, above all, by giving it a theological motivation: 'Hence it is proven in the most manifest way that before creating heaven and earth, God had made paradise (*prius quam coelum et terram Deus faceret, paradisum ante condiderat*)' (ibid.).

It is possible that his decision was influenced by the fact, which is likewise not easily explainable, that the Septuagint, which in Genesis 2:8, 2:10 and 4:16 keeps Eden as a place name, elsewhere translates Eden with *tryphē*, 'delight'. In any case, in the Latin Church's translation, paradise was already associated with pleasure, *locus voluptatis*, as we read in the Vulgate of Genesis 2:10 (and such will it be still for Dante: *delitiarum patria* [*De vulgari eloquentia* 1.7.2]). Humanity was created by God for pleasure—which was created, in its turn, before heaven and earth—but was later driven out of it for their guilt.

1.5. The earliest treatises on paradise, like that of Ephrem among the Greek fathers or that of Ambrose among the Latins, open with fear and trembling, as if the theme necessarily exceeded their powers. 'I was divided by a twofold affect,' writes Ephrem. 'On the one hand, the desire to know paradise, in order to explore its nature and properties, enraptured me; on the other, the terror of its difficulty and breadth drove me back' (*De paradiso Eden* 1[6].2). And yet, 'it is sweet to speak of paradise' (ibid. 1[6].8), to describe its magnificence, which exceeds every faculty of speaking: 'there sad February does not freeze, a glad temperance from heaven attenuates the strength of winter and the splendor of the sun trembles in a perpetual spring' (ibid. 10[15].2). The twelve months of the year are compared to tender brides: 'June there is like April, July mitigates its ardors with light breezes, and September spreads its copious dewdrops' (ibid.); the fertile soil, similar to a '*myrotheca* of aromas and perfumes' (ibid. 12[17].1), from its full bosom 'pours forth its flowers all year' (ibid. 10[15].3). What is decisive is that, in Ephrem, the earthly paradise is not yet divided from the celestial: 'while you are living, make for yourself the key to paradise: that door desires you and gladly expects your arrival' (ibid. 2[7].2).

For his part, Ambrose too, though articulating the problem technically in terms of the rhetorical tradition in which he had been educated ('what paradise is, where and in what way it is', *quidam sit paradisus, et ubi qualisve sit* [*De paradiso* 1.1]), betrays a 'burning [*aestum*] apprehension' before a theme of which not even Paul, who had been ecstatically enraptured there, had shown himself capable of speaking. The fact is that while the bishops were occupied almost exclusively in the councils with discussing the nature of God and the relations among the persons of the trinity, the problem of the nature and destiny of humanity remained decisively at the margins of theological discourse. It is on these margins that the theme of the earthly paradise intersects with that of human nature and its lot, until it finds some decades later with Augustine its classical locus in the doctrine of original sin.

This is evident in Ambrose. He inherits from Philo, probably through Origen's mediation, an exegetical tradition that interprets paradise as an allegory of the human soul. 'Paradise is a fertile land,' he writes, 'which is to say, the fruitful soul, planted in Eden, meaning in pleasure' (*Est ergo paradisus terra quaedam fertile, hoc est anima foecunda, in Eden plantata, hoc est in voluptate* [*De paradiso* 3.12]). Developing Philo's suggestion, Adam and Eve are the two faculties of the soul: intellect (*nous*) and sensation (*aisthesis*). The spring that waters the garden is Christ and the four rivers into which it is divided are the four cardinal virtues and, at the same time, the four ages of sacred history. The ultimate virtue, justice, which corresponds to the age of the Gospel, is the most important, because 'nothing makes the human race happier than justice (*hominum genus nullo magis quam iustitia et aequitate laetetur*)' (ibid. 3.18). The Gospel is 'a figure of justice, because it is the virtue that works salvation in every believer' (ibid. 3.22). And man, 'who was in the earth in which he was molded', was placed in paradise 'so that it would be known that in this way he had received the divine spirit of virtue' (ibid. 4.24). Consequently, Ambrose understands the passage from Genesis 2:15 ('and he put him in the paradise of pleasure, so that he might work it and take care of it') in the sense that it is humanity's task to preserve 'the gift of the perfect nature and the grace of full virtue,' of which paradise is the figure (ibid. 4.25).

1.6. In this allegorical equation between paradise and human nature there appears *in nuce* what will become the specific theological content of the earthly paradise: the originary justice of the creature, its loss because of sin and its salvific recovery through Christ. In Ambrose, however, the sin of our progenitors is not a drama that irrevocably marks and breaks up human nature, but almost a strata-gem that leads it towards salvation. Certainly Adam, even if he did not yet possess the knowledge of good and evil, transgressed the command that had been given to him and is therefore culpable. The tree of good and evil had, how-ever, been placed at the centre of the garden so that man could know 'the excellence of the good' (*supereminentiam boni*): 'how, in fact, if there was no knowledge of good and evil, could we discern good from evil?' (ibid. 2.8). Even the devil was placed in the garden 'so that we would know that the malice of the devil can also be helpful to the salvation of humanity' (ibid. 2.9). The punishment that humanity receives does not involve its nature: 'Consider that the man was not cursed, but the serpent, and neither was the earth cursed, but "cursed in your works"' (ibid. 15.77). And just as human nature is not yet divided, so in Ambrose paradise too—as is obvious in the spare title *De paradiso*—is not yet split, as will happen later, into an earthly paradise (forever lost) and a heavenly paradise, far off in the future.

Yet sin casts a shadow on human nature, such that Ambrose can define Adam's life in the Garden as an *umbra vitae* (shadow of a life) and his immortality solely as the pledge of a future life:

> Man was thus either in the shadow of a life because of the future life, because our life on earth now is a shadow (*umbra est haec quae nunc nostra est vita in terra*), or in a sort of pledge of life (*in quodam pignore vitae*), because he was given breath by God. He therefore has a pledge of immortality [. . .]. Even if he was not yet a sinner, his nature was nevertheless not incorrupt and inviolable; he was not yet a sinner, but as one who would have sinned later. He was for that reason in the shadow of life, as one who sins is in the shadow of death (ibid. 5.29).

Here begins the process that will lead paradise to become, from a place of delight and originary justice, nothing but the ambiguous backdrop of sin and corruption.

1.7. 'And he drove out the man and set before the paradise of delight cherubim and flaming swords, to guard the entrance to the tree of life' (Genesis 3:24). That what is decisive in the narration of Genesis is not so much the Garden as the expulsion from it—on this, the tradition, with some significant exceptions, is unanimous. Paradise is, certainly, the originary dwelling place of man (*de loco hominis* is the title of *quaestio* 102 of the *Summa Theologica* 1a, in which Aquinas responds positively to the question 'whether paradise is the place that was appropriate to man in his originary state'), but what is essential is not so much his sojourn in the 'abode of delights' (*sedes deliciarum*) that was destined to him—of brief duration, after all, six hours according to the prevailing interpretation—as the fact that he has been driven out of it *in istum miserarium locum* (into this place of miseries). Man is the living being that has been expelled from his own dwelling place, who has lost his originary place. He is on earth doubly *peregrinus*: not only because his eternal life will be in the celestial paradise, but also and above all because he has been exiled from his Edenic homeland.

For this reason it has been possible to affirm that not paradise, but its loss constitutes the original mythologeme of Western culture, a sort of originary traumatism that has profoundly marked Christian and modern culture, condemning to failure every search for happiness on earth.

A terrible metaphysical prohibition or a devastating psychological inhibition has made its mark on the imaginary of medieval and modern man, as if, at a certain moment of his history, a cataclysm had destroyed his hopes of a blessed life here and now, in the immediacy of his human condition (Braga 2004: 1).

'Cataclysm' and 'devastating psychological inhibition' remain metaphors as long as one does not attempt to reconstruct and comprehend the effective mechanisms and the strategic apparatuses by means of which Christian theology conceptually articulated the expulsion from paradise, in order to make of it the determinative event of the human condition and the foundation of its economy of salvation.

✿

2

The Sin of Nature

2.1. The most implacable of these apparatuses is certainly the doctrine of original sin, namely, of a sin that incurably corrupts human nature itself. Scholars debate still today whether it should be considered as Augustine's invention or to what extent it instead had patristic and scriptural precedents. The insistence with which Augustine—citing, and not always faithfully, Hilary (in reality, Ambrosiaster), Ambrose and Cyprian—suggests that his doctrine was always that of the Catholic Church, denying (contrary to all evidence) having professed in the past a more nuanced opinion, allows us to think that he was actually aware of the novelty of his thesis.

Since this rests entirely on the interpretation of a passage from the Letter to the Romans (5:12), to such a degree that, responding to Julian (who had accused him of having changed his opinion), he can summarize his own doctrine by repeating almost to the letter the words of the apostle and affirming that he had from the beginning always held them for true (*ab initio conversionis meae sic tenui semper et teneo* [*Contra Iulianum* 6.12.39]), it will be fitting to carefully examine Augustine's exegetical strategy. In the Latin tradition of which he makes use, the passage reads: *Per unum hominem peccatum intravit in mundum et per peccatum mors et ita in omnes homines pertransiit, in quo omnes peccaverunt* ('Through one man sin entered into the world and through sin, death, and then it passed into all men, in which all men sinned'). What is decisive for Augustine is the interpretation of *in quo*, which he refers, apparently without hesitating, to Adam: 'in which (man) all sinned.'

Scholars have pointed out for some time that the corresponding expression in the original Greek—*eph' ō*—introduces a consequential clause and therefore means 'on the basis of which, by the effect of which', and refers presumably to the masculine term that immediately precedes it, namely, *thanatos* ('in consequence of death all have sinned' [Schreiner 2014: 273–4; Fitzmyer 1993: *passim*]).

Augustine—who, in *De peccatorum meritis et remissione* (412 CE), had considered as possible both the reference of *in quo* to Adam (*in quo* homine *omnes peccaverunt*) and to sin (*in quo* peccato *omnes peccaverunt*)—was perfectly aware of the complexity of the passage and in *Contra duas epistolas Pelagianorum* also examines the problem in detail also with reference to the Greek original. Polemicizing against the Pelagians, who affirm that 'through Adam death has been transmitted to us, not sin (*per Adam mortem ad nos transisse, non crimina*)', he asks:

> What then does the following phrase mean: 'in which all have sinned' (*in quo omnes peccaverunt*)? Either the apostle wants to say that in that one man—of whom he had said, 'through one man sin entered the world'—all have sinned, or he means 'in which sin' or certainly 'in which death'. We must not worry that he has not written 'in which [*fem.*]' (*in qua*), but 'in which [*masc.*] all have sinned';[1] death in Greek is actually masculine in gender (*Contra duas epistolas Pelagianorum*, 4.4.7).

Even though Augustine appears to be aware of the grammatical reasons for the reference of *in quo* to death,

---

1 Italian is able to distinguish between the grammatical gender implied by the phrase 'in which' in a way that English is not [Trans.].

nevertheless at this point, with an abrupt reversal, he seeks instead to exclude this interpretation at all costs, in order to insinuate his own in its place:

> Either it is said that 'in that man all sinned', because, when he sinned, all were in him; or in that sin all sinned, because in a general way it became the sin of all, which all had to contract at the moment of birth; or it remains that they may say that in that death all sinned. But I do not see how this can be understood correctly. Men die in sin, they do not sin in death (*in peccato enim moriuntur homines, non in morte peccant*); indeed death follows upon a sin that precedes it, not sin upon death. 'The sting of death is sin', that is, the sting that produces death by its stinging, not the sting with which death stings us, just as poison, once drunk, is called the drink of death, because death is produced by it and not because this drink is produced or given by death. And if, in these words of the apostle, it cannot have meant sin, in which all have died, because in Greek, from which the letter has been translated, sin is feminine in gender, it remains that it may be understood that in that first man all have sinned, because all were in him when

he sinned; through which sin is contracted by being born, and only by being reborn can it be cancelled (*unde peccatum nascendo trahitur, quod nisi renascendo non solvitur*) (ibid.).

Not only does Augustine twist the interpretation of 1 Corinthians 15:16 ('The sting of death is sin'), in which both the general context and the immediately preceding verse ('O death, where is your sting?') seem to imply that the sting belongs to death and not that death is its product, but, moreover, grammatical reasons, which previously legitimated the reference to death, serve now to exclude the view that what is in question could be sin and allow one sole possible interpretation to survive, in which Adam's sin contaminates human nature itself and becomes the 'original sin' of all humanity.

2.2. Before confronting the deep motivations of Augustine's strategies, it will be opportune to examine his scriptural arguments, which prove to be at least weak, if not tendentious. The fact is that Augustine must contend not only with the Pelagian thesis, but with an exegetical tradition that excluded the transmission of Adam's sin to human nature and interpreted the Pauline *eph' ō* in reference to death.

Already Origen, while commenting on the Pauline passage, read it in such a way that there was not a trace of an original sin in Augustine's sense. In the first place, as has been suggested (Hammond Bammel 1985: 335), he read the *eph' ō* as causative ('for this reason', in an absolute sense or in reference to death). He also interprets *omnes peccaverunt* in the sense that, in consequence of the first sin, in every man there is constituted an 'image of Adam's transgression' (*similitudinem praevaricationis Adae in unoquoque*) (Origen 1992–93: 94) which, 'like a slight contagion' (*levi contagione*), drives them to sin. For this reason he distinguishes between those who already have this slight contagion and remain capable of not sinning, and those who instead voluntarily repeat Adam's sin:

Death entered into the world and passed into all, but did not rule in all. Indeed it is one thing to pass (*pertransire*), another to rule. Sin passed also into the just, and compels them with a slight contagion. In liars, by contrast, which is to say in those who have submitted to sin with all their mind and all their devotion, it rules and dominates them with all its power (ibid.: 68).

The rule of death is therefore not absolute: 'From Adam alone did sin begin to rule in this way, and it ruled in those who followed in the similitude (*similitudo* here means model or example) of Adam' (ibid.: 90).

Sin is not in fact a substance that could be transmitted, but consists only in works and gestures (*ipsum peccatum nec subsistit, quippe cum nec substantia sit eius usquam sit nisi in opere et gestis* [ibid.: 92]). If there is something like an originary contamination, it is not due to a transmission of sin by a natural transfer, but by a sort of fall that is repeated in each person, as if every person were each time driven from paradise 'in some inexpressible way' (*quodlibet inenarrabili modo et soli Deo cognito unusquisque de paradiso trusus videtur et exceptione condemnatur*). In writing 'Sin will not rule in your mortal body' (Romans 6:12), the apostle wanted to specify that grace rules in the same body that sin has rendered mortal (Origen 1992–93: 194). In any case, Origen reads the clear Pauline affirmations, according to which 'the gift is not like the crime' and 'where sin was abundant, grace was superabundant', in the sense that human nature is restored in its fullness: 'the grace by means of which justice rules in life', and 'where death was, there is eternal life' (ibid.: 124).

That from Adam humanity had inherited death, and sin solely through death, is the central idea of the *Commentary on the Letter to the Romans* of the Syrian bishop

Theodoret of Cyrus. Death produces need and need generates sin:

> Adam, subjected to the penalty of death, begot
> Cain and Seth and others. And all, having been
> begotten by such a man, had a mortal nature. And
> this had need of many things: food, water, clothing, houses, and technical skills. The use of such
> things drives the impulses of the soul to incontinence and incontinence begets sin. For this reason
> the divine apostle affirms that, Adam having
> sinned and being subjected to death because of
> sin, diffuses both the one and the other in the
> human race: 'indeed death reaches all men and
> through it (*eph' ō*) all commit sin' (Theodoret 1998:
> 103–04).

There is therefore no transmission of an original sin,
but every person sins anew because of his mortal condition: 'Each bears upon himself the limit of death not for
the sin of the first man, but for his own sin' (ibid.).

ℵ. Origen, according to what we can deduce from Rufinus' Latin
translation, which has preserved for us his commentary on the
Letter to the Romans, read the text of 5:14 in this way: *Usque ad*

legem enim peccatum erat in hoc mundo. Peccatum autem non imputatur, cum lex non est. Sed regnavit mors ab Adam usque ad Moysen in eos qui peccaverunt in similitudinem praevaricationis Adae, qui est forma futuri ('Up to the time of the law sin was in this world. Sin, however, is not imputed, when there is no law. But death ruled from Adam until Mòses in those who sinned in similitude to the offence of Adam, who is the form of the one to come'); but, being the good philologist that he was, he knew that there were codices that contained the reading *in eos, qui non peccaverunt* ('in those who did *not* sin). According to Origen, it is necessary to distinguish the *pertransire* (transmitting) of death from its *regnare* (ruling):

> Death entered into the world and passed into all, but it did not rule in all. Indeed it is one thing to pass, another to rule. Sin passed also into the just, and constrained them with a slight contagion. In liars, by contrast, which is to say in those who have submitted to sin with all their mind and all their devotion, it rules and dominates them with all its power (1992–93: 68).

But even in this case his interpretation does not change substantially: even the just who did not sin are under the law of death, but they are liberated from it by Christ. In his commentary on Romans 5:12, Origen affirms moreover the innocence of the *parvuli* as long as they have not acquired reason. Thus he interprets Paul's phrase: *Ego autem vivebam aliquando sine peccato, hoc est: in puerili aetate* ('Indeed I once lived without sin, that is: in the age of childhood' [ibid.: 60]).

2.3. It is precisely in the text that Augustine cites most often in support of his thesis that the tendentiousness of his exegesis clearly appears. Immediately after the passage cited from *Contra duas epistolas Pelagianorum*, Augustine adds:

> *Nam sic et sanctus Hilarius intellexit quod scriptum est 'In quo omnes peccaverunt'; ait enim: 'In quo, id est Adam, omnes peccaverunt.' Deinde addidit: 'Manefestum in Adam omnes peccasse quasi in massa; ipse enim per peccatum corruptus, omnes quos genuit nati sunt sub peccato.' Haec scribens Hilarius sine ambiguitate commonuit, quomodo intellegendum esset: 'In quo omnes peccaverunt'.* (For thus Saint Hilary also understands why it is written 'In which all have sinned'; he says therefore: 'In which, that is Adam, all have sinned.' Then he adds: 'It is obvious that in Adam all sinned as if in a mass; being himself corrupted by sin, all those whom he begets are born under sin.' In writing this Hillary reminds us unambiguously in what way 'In which all have sinned' is to be understood.) (4.4.7)

Modern scholars have demonstrated for some time now that the text that Augustine is citing is not from Hilary but comes from the commentary on the Letter to the

Romans that, since the time of Erasmus, it has been customary to designate as Ambrosiaster (or pseudo-Ambrose). It is sufficient to restore the citation to the context from which Augustine has extracted it to understand that it not only is not *sine ambiguitate* but says in part the contrary of what Augustine is making it say. In Ambrosiaster's text the citation from Augustine in fact continues: *ideo dixit 'in quo', cum de muliere loquatur, quia non ad speciem retulit sed ad genus* ('indeed he said "in which [*masc.*]", when he was speaking of the woman, since he is referring not to a specific person but to the race' [1966: 165; 2009: 40]). The problem that the anonymous author has in view is that of the attribution to Eve of responsibility for death (*per illam mors intravit in mundum*, 'through her death entered into the world'). Paul had written *in quo* instead of *in qua* because—according to a procedure that Augustine elsewhere demonstrates that he is familiar with (*De doctrina christiana* 3.34.48)—though having Eve in mind (*cum de muliere loquatur*), he refers not to the specific person but to the race. It has been fittingly suggested that, if Augustine has truncated the citation, it is perhaps because precisely this thesis of Ambrosiaster was contrary to his doctrine according to which the human race derives from Adam alone (the woman was created from the body of Adam to show that *omnino ex homine uno diffunderetur genus humanum*, 'entirely from one man is the human race propagated' [*De civitate Dei* 12.21]).

But the rest of the citation as well, once restored to its context, acquires another meaning and joins in some way the exegetical tradition that, against Augustine's reading, refers the *in quo* to death. In specifying the sense of *per peccatum corruptus*, the anonymous author in fact affirms that the corruption that Adam transmits to his descendants is not sin, but bodily death. Beyond this, he adds:

> there is also another death that is called second in Hell and that we do not undergo through the sin of Adam, but it is acquired with our own sins, to which the former furnishes the occasion (*quam non peccato Adae patimur, sed eius occasione propriis peccatis adquiritur*). From this death the good are immune (Ambrosiaster 1966: 163; 2009: 40).

The contradiction with the doctrine of original sin is so obvious that theologians have hypothesized that Augustine had found the text that he attributes to Hilary in a collection of *Testimonia* that contained only fragments. In any case, Ambrosiaster's text, in which some historians of religion have seen the model for the Augustinian theory, constitutes instead a point-by-point denial of it.

2.4. In Augustine's strategy, ecclesial reasons overlap so closely with theological ones that the latter become indistinguishable from the former. In the writings against the Pelagians, in which Augustine elaborates his doctrine of original sin, what is actually in question is above all the necessity of the baptism of *parvuli* (just as, in the polemic with the Donatists, it is the validity of baptism conferred by bishops *traditores*, who had, that is to say, handed over holy books to the Roman authorities). It is in order to combat the thesis that Caelestius refuses to anathematize, according to which 'Adam's sin damaged only him [. . .] and infants are at the moment of birth in the same state in which Adam was before his transgression' (*De gratia Christi et de peccato originali*, 2.2.2), that Augustine realizes that he has to implicate human nature itself in sin. And the reason that he advances above all is that 'if human nature can be just, then Christ has died in vain' (*Si per naturam iustitia, ergo Christus gratis mortuus est*) (*De natura et gratia* 2.2), which is to say, in ecclesial terms, the sacraments—in this case, baptism—are not necessary. For this reason, with pitiless tenacity, he must confirm again and again—in pages that are certainly not edifying—that infants who could not be baptized are irredeemably damned:

I therefore affirm that the infant born in a place in which it could not be baptized because death impeded it and it has thus left this life without the bath of regeneration. [. . .] justly, because of the condemnation that runs through the whole mass of humanity (*quae per universam massam currit*), this infant will not be admitted into the kingdom of heaven, even if it could not in any way be Christian (ibid. 8.9).

And he immediately adds, so that it is clear what is at stake in the Pelagian negation of original sin:

I am not speaking only of an infant: if a youth or an old person dies in a region in which no one has been able to hear the name of Christ, can they perhaps be just through their nature and their free will? If that is affirmed, it means rendering vain the cross of Christ (*crucem Christi evacuare*) (ibid. 9.10).

What is thus devoid of sense is not so much the cross as the catholicity and necessity of the Church and its sacraments.

2.5. From a strictly theological point of view, the innovation —hence its strength and, at the same time, its weakness—

of Augustine's thesis is that of implicating in sin not only the human person, but his very nature and his very life.

> The wound that we call sin wounds life itself, by which it is rightly lived (*ipsam vitam vulnerat, qua recte vivebatur*). [. . .] By way of this great sin of the first man, our nature has been changed for the worse and has not only become sinful, but has also generated sinners (*natura ibi nostra in deterius commutata, non solum est facta peccatrix, verum etiam genuit peccatores*) (*De nuptiis et concupiscientia* 2.34.57).

The paradox inherent in the notion of original sin—which makes it a unique case in the history of Western ethics—is that what is culpable is not the action of a single person nor its repetition on the part of a collectivity, but the *natura hominis* as such *facta peccatrix*, life itself in all its functions—including, above all, the reproductive function. The thesis is all the more difficult to sustain insofar as, to avoid falling into Manicheanism, Augustine must deny that nature is evil in itself and confirm that sin is not a nature but a vice (*non est utique natura, sed vitium* [ibid.]); but, with that, one is wrapped up in obvious contradictions, because one cannot see how a vice can be unfailingly transmitted by birth. The contradiction is resolved by doubling the idea of nature and introducing into it, so to speak, a history: for an integral Edenic nature sin substitutes a *natura lapsa*, a fallen and corrupt nature.

> We do not accuse the nature of the soul or the body, which is created by God and is entirely good (*quam Deus creavit et quae tota bona est*); but we say that it has been corrupted by its own will (*propria voluntate vitiata*) and cannot be healed without God's grace (*De perfectione iustitiae hominis* 6.12).

But even after regeneration through the work of baptism, the corruption of nature remains in the form of the concupiscence that incurably drives man to sin (*Nam cum est adhuc aliquid carnalis concupiscentiae* [. . .] *non omni modo ex tota anima diligitur Deus* [ibid. 8.19]; *Ecce et baptizatis caro invenitur esse contraria et non adesse possibilitas illa, quam inseparabiliter insitam dicit esse naturae* [*De natura et gratia* 53.61]).

This means on closer inspection—hence further difficulties—attributing to the human will the unheard-of capacity to transform the nature created by God. The expulsion from paradise acquires from this perspective its true meaning: man is the living being that can corrupt his nature, but not heal it, thus consigning himself to a history and to an economy of salvation, in which the divine grace dispensed by the Church through its sacraments becomes essential.

2.6. In the face of such a contradictory notion, the objections of Pelagius and Caelestius, which Augustine always cites to refute them, are actually in a good position. If sin, as Augustine also concedes, is not a substance, but an act, 'how could what is deprived of substance corrupt or change human nature?' (*quomodo potuit humanam debilitare vel mutare naturam, quod substantia caret* [ibid. 19.21]). And if sin becomes, as in the doctrine of original sin, something necessary that cannot be avoided, then it is not truly a sin; if it instead depends on the will, then it can be avoided, and man can then—at least virtually—be without sin (*si quod vitari potest, potest homo sine peccato esse, quod vitari potest* [*De perfectione iustitiae hominis* 2.1]). But above all it is with respect to the cornerstone of Augustine's doctrine—the absolute impossibility for man to save himself without grace—that Pelagius' criticisms seem especially pertinent. Pelagius does not in fact deny grace but the opposition between grace and nature. 'Grace,' he affirms, 'is precisely the possibility not to sin, which our nature receives from God, insofar as it was created with free will.' That is to say, grace inheres in human nature as an inseparable (or *inadmissible*, according to the neologism that Augustine coins to critique Pelagius) possibility, and if all that concerns our nature derives from the one who created it, 'how could that which belongs properly to God put itself forward as deprived of the grace of God?' (*De nature et gratia* 51.59).

Once again, against these clear theses, Augustine must have recourse to the doubling of human nature worked out by sin: the possibility that was available to man in the paradisiac condition was lost when his nature was corrupted and estranged itself from grace, which he now needs, like a sick body, as a remedy. This and nothing else is the meaning of original sin.

א. In the implacable conflict with Pelagius, what is at stake for Augustine is the distinction between nature and grace, which he wants at every cost to save. If, as Pelagius does, one denies original sin, if one affirms that man has been given with his nature the possibility of not sinning, then grace becomes superfluous. Pelagius' error, that is to say, is that of confusing nature and grace, of attributing to nature what lies solely in the province of grace. 'This one could in some way accept,' writes Augustine,

> if one understood the human nature that was created unscathed and without fault [. . .] but it should not be said in any way of the nature which was able to be corrupted and to have need of a doctor, that his blind eyes may be healed and sight restored to them (ibid.).

After sin, human nature is in fact incurably corrupt and grace is to it like medicine to the ill.

We do not have power either over our hearts or over our thoughts, which when suddenly clouded confuse the mind and the soul, drawing them far from what we have intended. They look back on things of the world, they insinuate into everything what is worldly, they tempt the will, they plot seductions, and in the very instant when we seek to lift up our mind, vain thoughts throw us back down toward earthly things. Who is so happy as to be able always to lift up his heart? And who can do it without the help of God? No one, absolutely (*Contra duas epistolas Pelagianorum* 4.11.30).

Yet again, theological reasons coincide in Augustine with ecclesial ones: if human nature were capable of not sinning without grace, then the Church, which dispenses it through its sacraments, would not be necessary.

2.7. At the beginning of his treatise *De conceptu virginali et de originali peccato* (On the Virgin Conception and Original Sin), Anselm picks up Augustine's doctrine, but he introduces into it an important distinction, which will have a long lineage. To explain how God could have assumed in Christ 'a man without sin from the sinful mass of the human race' (*hominem assumpsit de generis humani massa peccatrice sine peccato*), he firmly distinguishes between personal sin and original sin. 'It is not doubted,' he writes, that the term 'original' comes from 'origin'. If original sin is only in man, it will be called such either from the origin of human nature, namely from his original beginning, insofar as he derives from the human origin itself (*ab ipsa humanae naturae origine trahatur*); or from the origin, which is to say from the beginning of each person, because he derives by origin from this. But it does not seem to derive from the beginning of human nature, because its origin was just, since the progenitors were created just, without sin. It seems thus that it is called original from the very origin of each human person (Anselm 1990: 136; 1998: 359).

The distinction is decisive, because it implies for Anselm that original sin, while deriving in every person from the Edenic progenitors from whom they draw their nature, acquires reality only with the origin—in other words, with the birth—of each person.

If anyone says that the sin is called original, because it descends to individuals from those from whom they receive the origin of their nature, I will not contradict him, on the condition, however, that he not deny that original sin is transmitted (literally 'is carried') with the origin of each person (*originale peccatum cum ipsa uniuscuiusque personae origine trahi*). Although, in fact, in each man there is at the same time (*simul*) both the nature through which he is a man like others and the person through which he is differentiated from them, so that he is called 'this' or 'that' and called by name, such as Adam or Abel, the sin of each is in his nature and in his person (for the sin of Adam was in man, which is to say in his nature, and in the one who was called Adam, which is to say in his person). There is however a sin that each one bears (*trahit*) with his nature in his very origin, and a sin that he bears not with his nature, but he himself commits it, when he is already a person different from others. That sin which is assumed in the origin itself is called 'original' and can also be called 'natural', not because it belongs to the essence of his nature, but because it is assumed together with it because of its corruption (*non quod sit ex essentia naturae, sed quoniam propter eius corruptionem cum illa assumitur*). As for the sin that each commits once he has become a person (*postquam persona est*), one can call it 'personal', because it comes from that person's vice. For the same reason, justice can be called original and personal, because Adam and Eve originally, which is to say in their very beginning, as soon as they existed as humans were just at the same time and without interval (*simul sine intervallo iusti fuerunt*). By contrast, one can call 'personal' that justice that the unjust person receives without having it originally (ibid.: 138; 1998: 359–60).

This distinction, with which Anselm means to clarify the obscurity of Augustine's doctrine, actually does nothing but render the contradictions more explicit. If the progenitors' sin can only be a personal sin (Adam and Eve, he specifies, *personaliter peccaverunt*), why did there then belong to it the power to contaminate and alter human nature itself and transform itself in this way into original sin in individual human beings? A 'natural' sin in truth cannot exist: as Anselm takes care to specify, if it is called 'natural', it is certainly not because it belongs to the essence of human nature, but only because it is a personal sin that is assumed by way of its corruption (*propter eius corruptionem*). What is original is not, therefore, the sin, but the corruption that the nature has inexplicably received from a sin that is and remains personal. Augustine and Anselm's doctrine, which the Church has accepted without benefit of an inventory, is a doctrine not of original sin but of the *originalis corruptio* of human nature, for which the sin furnishes the pretext.

From this perspective, the fact that nature and person are distinguished and, at the same time, trade places with each other in a sort of shell game is particularly obvious when Anselm takes up the doctrine of the two sins to justify the original stain of infants. 'Just as the personal (sin),' he writes, 'crosses to nature, so natural (sin) crosses to the person (*Et sicut personale transit ad naturam, ita naturale ad personam*)' (1990: 186; 1998: 382). That Adam ate from the tree of the garden was a natural necessity; but that he ate the fruit from the prohibited tree was, by contrast, a personal act of will. And yet nature, which has thus been excluded from the voluntary act, is immediately afterwards included in it as the obscure bearer of guilt, which transforms the personal act into a sin that concerns the whole human race (*Quod Adam comedebat, hoc natura exigebat, quia ita ut hoc exigeret creata erat. Quod vero de ligno vetito comedit, non hoc voluntas naturalis, sed personalis, id est propria, fecit. Quod tamen fecit persona, non fecit sine natura. Persona enim erat quod dicebatur Adam; natura, quod homo. Fecit igitur persona peccatricem naturam, quia cum Adam peccavit, homo peccavit*) (ibid.). 'In this way,' Anselm can conclude, 'Adam's personal sin crosses over into all those who are naturally propagated from him and becomes in them original or natural (*Hoc modo transit pecca-tum Adae personale in omnes qui de illo naturaliter propagantur et est in illis originale sive naturale*)' (ibid.). The person, which renders imputable to the individual man Adam a guilt that nature cannot commit, is converted immediately into nature, thus rendering all of humanity co-responsible for this guilt and transforming it into a *massa perditionis*.

ℵ. Since what is in question is the attempt to transform a personal sin into a natural guilt, it is not surprising that, both in Anselm and in Augustine, the vocabulary of original sin should be of a vegetal order. From this perspective, the use of the verb *propagare* as a technical term for the transmission of sin is instructive: *propagare* originally means 'to plant a seedling' and *propago* is the sprout or sucker that emerges from a shrub (Anselm: *Sicut itaque* [human nature] *si non peccasset, qualis facta est a deo talis propagaretur, ita post peccatum qualem se peccando facit talis propagatur*, 'If human nature had not sinned, it would have been propagated as God had made it: thus after its sin it is propagated according to what it has made of itself by sinning' [1990: 138; 1998: 360]). In the same sense, Augustine compares the man who receives divine grace to an *arbor bona* (good tree) and the one who corrupts human nature with sin to a *mala arbor* (evil tree). And it is certainly not an accident if Pelagius takes aim at precisely this vegetal metaphor, affirming that the sin of Adam has been diffused in the human race *non propagine, sed exemplo* (not by propagation but by example), which is to say, not in a natural but in a personal way.

2.8. The apparatus that permits one to think the degeneration of human nature as a whole through the sin of one alone is the term 'mass'. It is likely that Augustine drew it from the passage cited from Ambrosiaster (*omnes in Adamo peccasse quasi in massa*), even if a clear New Testament precedent was in Romans 9:21, where the word *phyrama*, translated into Latin with *massa*, does not have, however, any negative connotation and designates the clay with which the potter forms all his pots: 'Does the potter not have the power to make from the same lump of earth (*luti ex eadem massa*) a pot for an honorable use and one for a dishonorable use?'

Augustine develops the Pauline concept in an autonomous way, referring it to human nature as constituted as a result of Adam's sin into a single *massa perditionis* (mass of damnation). What is decisive, in fact, is that the mass is not here, as in Paul, something preexisting, but comes into being with sin, as if this latter were somehow given a creative power: *ab illa perditionis massa, quae facta est per hominum primum* ('from this mass of damnation, which was made by the first man') (*Enchiridion* 23.92). In *De gratia Christi et de peccato originali* the expression recurs in this sense two times, first to interpret the Pauline saying in Romans 5:12:

> From the moment, then, in which 'through one
> man sin entered into the world and with sin,
> death, which therefore passed into all men,
> through whom all sinned', clearly the whole mass
> of damnation has become possessed by the one
> who lost it (*universa massa perditionis facta est possessio
> perditoris*) (2.29.34).

and second to motivate the damnation of infants who die
without baptism:

> How is the infant justly punished with damnation,
> if not because it is part of the mass of damnation
> (*nisi quia pertinet ad massam perditionis*) and, as born
> of Adam, is justly condemned by the ancient debt,
> unless he is liberated, not by having paid it, but by
> grace? (ibid. 2.31.36)

But already in earlier writings, the idea of a *massa* is
closely linked to original sin. Commenting on the passage
in Romans 9:21, in *De diversis quaestionibus* (68.3), Augustine
evokes the fall of Adam, in whom *natura nostra peccavit* (our
nature sinned), and draws from it the consequence that
since then, Providence no longer forms human beings
according to a divine prototype, but from a *massa luti* (mass
of clay), which in reality is a *massa peccati* (mass of sin). And

in *Ad Simplicianum*, humanity (the *genus humanum*) appears several times as 'a single mass of sin (*una quaedam massa peccati*)' (1.2.16), constituted by Adam in its totality as 'one sole mass of all men, which is transmitted through the transfer of sin and through the penalty of death (*tunc facta est una massa omnium, veniens de traduce peccati et de poena mortalitatis*)' (ibid. 1.2.20).

It has been observed that, in Augustine's usage, the idea of origin is more important than that of number, which by contrast defines the modern meaning of the term 'mass'. In reality the two senses are closely implicated, to the point of becoming indiscernible. The mass of sin coincides with human nature and this latter is *una massa omnium* (one mass of all), both constitutive principle and numerical totality of sinners (*massa peccatorum*). This is so much the case that, in his writings on predestination, the term, when it is connected to the theme of the inscrutable divine election, defines above all a numerical set—thus in *De dono perseverantiae* (14.35), the non-elect, as also the Jews who did not believe, are left in the same 'mass of perdition' as the pagans (*ubi nisi in massa perditionis iusto divino iudicio relinquuntur, ubi Tyrii relicti sunt et Sidonii* [. . .]. *In eadem perditionis massa relicti sunt etiam Iudaei, qui non potuerunt credere*); and in the last books of *De civitate Dei* as well, while the elect obtain

salvation, the rest, as part of the *massa damnata*, is abandoned to damnation.

‎א. In Augustine, the term *massa*, insofar as it designates the condition
—at once historical and theological—of the human race after the
fall, in some way constitutes a theological-political paradigm and it
should therefore not be surprising that it reappears in modernity precisely in this sense. The Schmittian principle according to which all
modern political categories are secularized theological categories
here finds a particularly meaningful application. In the course of the
nineteenth century up to the moment when, in 1923, José Ortega y
Gasset diagnosed its irreversible triumph, 'the mass' or 'the masses'
appear ever more often as the new sovereign subject, which is progressively substituted for the people—and here it is not important
whether it is greeted, on the right or the left of the array of parties,
as a positive phenomenon or as the worst of catastrophes.

Already in the New Testament's usage, the Greek term for
'people' (*demos*) despite being so important in the political tradition
of the West, almost never appears. In its place, we encounter the
words *ochlos* (175 occurrences), translated into Latin as *turba* or *plebs*
(the translation as 'mass' in the modern sense would clearly not be
illegitimate), *plethos* ('multitude') and *laos*, a more neutral term than
demos. One can say that the mass (*massa peccatorum*) is the extreme
form that the people assumes from the impolitical perspective of
the economy of salvation. When, between the nineteenth and twentieth centuries, it is secularized in order to be constituted as the new

subject of political movements, its theological origin is not in any way belied. The *massa perditionis*, which, in Augustine's words, had become the possession of demonic powers (*possessio perditoris*), must now be liberated from these latter in order to affirm its dominion (this is the ultimate sense of the 'revolt of the masses'). And yet, once restored to the theological perspective from which they originate, the masses' repeated attempts at emancipation in our time could only fail. The *massa damnata*, insofar as it by definition cannot be liberated by itself, but only through a divine intervention, falls necessarily into the hands of leaders and parties that make use of it for their own ends. The political subject of the totalitarian movements of the twentieth century ends up in the horrors of camps and extermination.

2.9. In the Augustinian doctrine of original sin, what is in question above all is the meaning of the earthly paradise. If human nature has been corrupted and *in peius mutata* (changed for the worse), if man has been for this reason irrevocably expelled from his originary homeland and will no longer be able to have access to it, then it is the very meaning of the *situs deliciarum* (site of pleasures) that has to be called into question. The Garden planted in Eden, with its trees, its plants 'pleasing to the eye and good for food' and its four rivers, insofar as it concerns a lost nature that will never be recuperated as such, can no longer have any meaning for humanity and, if it survives, it survives uselessly.

In Augustine's exegetical practice, this awareness is expressed in his radical change in the interpretation of the corresponding passages from Genesis. At an earlier time, when the doctrine of original sin had not yet been completely elaborated, he had composed a commentary in two books (*De Genesi contra Manichaeos*) in which paradise and its trees were interpreted allegorically as a figure of the *beatitudo hominis* ('happiness of man'—*his verbis etiam spirituales deliciae, quas habet beata vita, figurate explicantur* [2.9.12]). From this perspective, even sin and the consequent driving away from paradise did not appear as a definitive corruption of human nature and an incurable exile, but as a good recuperable through patience and love. Commenting on the passage on the expulsion, where he read *dismisit illum de paradiso* in the Latin translation, he writes:

> *Bene dictum est 'dimisit', non, 'exclusit'* [. . .]. *Potest ergo videri propterea homo in labores huius vitae esse dimissus, ut aliquando manum porrigat ad aborem vitae, ut vivat in aeternum.* (It is well said as 'dismiss', not 'exclude' [. . .]. It seems in fact that man has been dismissed into the toils of this life, so that he can

reach out his hand toward the tree of life and live eternally.) (ibid. 2.22.34)

One could have access to the tree of life—he concludes—not only through bearing earthly penalties (*per tolerantiam temporalium molestiae*) but also through love (*per caritatem*) (ibid. 2.23.26).

When, many years later, he writes his—thus the title emphasizes—literal commentary on Genesis (*De Genesi ad litteram*), the exegetical strategy changes radically. If in the past, he notifies us at the beginning, immediately after his conversion, he had interpreted in a figural sense the events for which he did not succeed in finding the literal sense, 'now the Lord has willed that, by looking deeper within and considering more closely these texts, I should also show that these facts had been written in a proper sense and not in an allegorical sense' (8.2.5). From this new perspective, which coincides with the polemic against Pelagius and the elaboration of the doctrine of original sin, 'paradise, where God placed man, is nothing other than a certain locality on the earth, where an earthly man could live (*nihil aliud quam locus quidam intellegatur terrae scilicet ubi habitaret homo terrenus*) (ibid. 8.1.1). This disenchanted refusal of all allegorical reading of the biblical text is all the more significant insofar as it denies an exegetical tradition that, starting from Philo and Origen, had profoundly influenced Ambrose, whom Augustine considered his master and who had seen in paradise an allegory of the human soul and in the tree of life an image of wisdom. Against this tradition, Augustine invites us not to neglect what appears *ante oculos* (before our eyes):

> Man was put in paradise to cultivate it, by means of an agricultural labor that was not toilsome, but joyous [. . .] and to watch over it, taking care not to commit any act by which he would merit being expelled from it. For this reason he received a precept, by observing which he would never have been expelled (ibid. 8.10.22).

To the corruption of *natura lapsa* (fallen nature) through sin there corresponds in Augustine the necessity of hell. In *De civitate Dei* (21.17ff.), he refutes those (ironically called the 'merciful') who, beginning with Origen, think that God will not eternally maintain the punishments of hell or that, even more, at the moment of the Judgement all the damned will be saved (or, at least, a part of them: the baptized or those who remained in the Church up to the end or practised alms). 'Since the eternal life of the saints will be without end, doubless the eternal chastisement of the damned will also not have an end.' Augustine gives no argument other than the words of scripture (Matthew 25:41: 'Depart, far from me, cursed ones, into the eternal fire prepared for the devil and his angels'); but the true argument is that the corrupted nature cannot disappear and be healed forever. If it could have been completely healed, then original sin could also have been completely redeemed and cancelled. For this reason, to the ontological split of human nature there must correspond, on the one hand, a forever empty earthly paradise and a heavenly paradise for the elect and, on the other, a hell where the *natura lapsa* will survive eternally.

2.10. Augustine realizes that, once interpreted literally, the story of Genesis 2 and 3 would have no sense other than that of serving as an introduction to the transgression that, by splitting human nature in two, constitutes paradise into a past that is forever lost. In the eleventh book of his commentary, at the moment when he takes leave of the work (the twelfth book, dedicated to the paradise into which Paul says he was enraptured, was added later), in reference to the literal interpretation of the final verse ('And he drove out Adam and placed before paradise of delight a cherub, with a flaming and turning sword to watch over the way to the tree of life'), Augustine cannot escape the impression that, with the exception of the fall, all that is said of the Garden seems 'done uselessly' (*frustra factum esse*), unless one surreptitiously introduces an allegorical allusion to the spiritual paradise (*nisi quia significat aliquid etiam de paradiso spirituali*) (*De Genesi ad litteram* 11.44.55).

With his *frustra factum est*, Augustine was a good prophet. The suspicion of the uselessness of what happens in paradise before and after the original sin was to be advanced many times in the history of theology and just as many times there was to be suggested an explanation as stereotypical as it is insufficient. A passage from the *Summa Theologica* can stand for all of them:

> A place in which no one lives is useless (*frustra est locus in quo nullum locatum continetur*), but after sin paradise is no longer a place of human habitation. Thus, if it was a place most suitable for human habitation, it was instituted by God in vain (1a, q. 102, a. 2, arg. 3).

The response that Aquinas gives—'in this way is shown the benevolence of God towards man and what they lost with their sin'—is certainly no more satisfying than that suggested by Augustine. If its only sense is that of having furnished the occasion for sin, for all that remains the Garden of delights was created uselessly. While the Kingdom to come is the central paradigm of the history of humanity, the Garden is deprived of any meaning whatsoever for that history.

א. From this perspective, one of the hidden motifs of Augustine's polemic against Pelagius concerns precisely the contemporary status of the Garden. If the human soul has preserved, according to the teaching of Pelagius and Caelestius, its possibility of not sinning, then man is in some way still in relation with the originary justice that he had possessed in paradise. It is this relation with the archetypal past of humanity that, for Augustine, must be cut off at all costs. Human nature has been irrevocably corrupted by Adam's sin and any presumption whatsoever to preserve a relation with Edenic justice is reprovable and illusory. By contrast, Pelagius never stops repeating that the possibility not to sin is the grace that human nature received at the moment of creation and that it preserves even after the Adamic transgression.

🌿

3

Man Has Never Yet Been in Paradise

3.1. If the Augustinian doctrine on original sin and the earthly paradise ended up prevailing in the tradition of the Church, there are nevertheless authors and moments in the history of medieval thought in which the Garden presents a very different image. We will linger in particular over two of these moments: Scotus Eriugena's *Periphyseon* and Dante's *Commedia*.

We cannot tackle the reading of the five books of Eriugena's work without the preliminary warning that we are dealing with an author to whom the considerations that Leo Strauss develops in connection with Moses Maimonides and Baruch Spinoza in *Persecution and the Art of Writing* are particularly appropriate. Since he knows that he is pronouncing absolutely new theses in theological material, he must multiply cautions, contradictions and obscurities, and, above all, orchestrate an impressive net of authoritative citations that were to guarantee his loyalty to the tradition of the Church. Nothing is more instructive, from this perspective, than his strategic use of Augustine's texts. One can say, in fact, that, beginning already with his youthful writing *On Predestination*, Eriugena consciously elaborated an anti-Augustinian theology. It is all the more urgent for him to proclaim his deference to this 'most holy and most divine theologian' (*Preiphyseon* 803B) and, through a learned weaving of citations, to disguise his obvious divergences as the attempt to reconcile the opinions of the Greeks, represented for him by Gregory of Nyssa, with those of the Romans, 'among whom none was of greater authority than Aurelius Augustine' (804D). The question becomes more pressing in book four, in which the reading of Genesis aims to refute, without ever openly admitting it, the Augustinian doctrine of original sin.

Already at the moment in the third book when he comments on Genesis 1:20 ('And God said: let the water produce the aquatic species of living soul and that which flies above the earth under the firmament of heaven'), Eriugena develops a theory of life of Platonic ancestry, but without counterpart in the thought of his time. Against those who affirm that 'the elements of the world, the heavens with their stars, the ether with the planets, the air with its clouds and its gusts of wind, thunderbolts, and other perturbations and even the water and its fluctuating motion lack not only soul, but also every kind of life' (728A), he recalls that

> Plato, the greatest among philosophers, and those who follow him, maintain not only that there is a general life of the world (*generalem mundi vitam*), but also that no species that adheres to a body and no body are deprived of life, and they have called this life a general soul or soul of the species (ibid.).

Here Eriugena introduces, alongside that of 'general life,' the notion of a 'vital motion' (*vitalis motus*), which permeates and animates every being and which no creature can lack:

> If [. . .] no substance can be deprived of vital motion, which maintains it and causes it to subsist, and every being that naturally moves receives the principle of its movement from life, it follows necessarily that every creature is life for itself or participates in life and is in some way alive (*aut per se*

ipsam vita sit, aut vitae particeps et quodam modo vivens) (728B).

This 'most general' life, suggests Eriugena with an obvious reference to Plato, 'is called most universal soul of the world by wise men and common life by those who investigate the divine Sophia' (729A). At this point, radicalizing the Platonic thesis, Eriugena extends this 'common life' even to death. Not only can no creature be deprived of life, but even bodies that to our senses appear dead are not, in reality, abandoned by life.

> Just as their composition and formation is the work of life, so also their dissolution, the loss of form and the return to the elements from which they were drawn is accomplished in obedience to the same principle [. . .] where, indeed, would life be when the body is dissolved, if not in that same dissolved body? Just as life is not composite in the composite, so it is not dissolved in the dissolved, nor reborn in the reborn, nor does it vivify what is joined together in its integrity more than what is disjoined into parts, nor is it greater, which is to say more powerful, in the whole than the part, nor lesser in the part than in the whole. The dissolution itself, which we call death of the body, is such

through our senses and through matter, not for nature itself, which remains inseparable in itself and is always whole in the same instant, and is not divided according to times and spaces (729C).

Consequently, human life also remains such forever: 'man does not cease to be man' (*homo non desinit esse homo*). And since man is body and soul, he will always be soul and body, 'even if the parts of the body are separated among themselves'.

The body of a man, whether it be living or dead, is the body of a man (*Corpus humanum, sive vivum, sive mortuum, corpus hominis est*). Similarly the human soul, whether it governs its own body united to itself, or ceases to govern it, as it seems to the senses, once dissolved into parts, does not cease to be the soul of a man (729D–730A).

Soul and life are, in Eriugena's usage, perfectly synonymous.

3.2. At this point it is on the analysis of human life that the philosopher concentrates his treatment. Taking up the Aristotelian distinction between vegetative, sensible, and intellectual life, Eriugena affirms that all three types of life are contained in man, but that they are actually one sole potential, which acts 'contemporaneously both in a general way in all human bodies and in a special way in individuals' (733D). With his customary boldness, he dwells particularly on precisely that life that was traditionally considered inferior to the others and that, insofar as it is deprived of intellect and sensibility, can seem to be almost 'a non-life or a non-soul' (734C): vegetative life, which he calls, to instead emphasize its vitality, 'germinal life' (*germinalis vita*). 'There is no need to consider as of small account,' he writes,

> this natural potential (*vis naturalis*), which nourishes and increases all the creatures that inhere in the earth with all their roots (*radicitus*) and are born from the earth according to the infinite number of shoots and grasses and produces in their own species and according to the resemblance of singular genuses the natural succession of flowers, fruits, and seeds (734D).

It is a matter, once again, of reaffirming the unity of life beyond its divisions:

> All the bodies that are found in the sensible universe are held together by vital motion (*vitali motu continentur*), whether they move or are immobile.

It is not surprising that Eriugena affirms at this point that the souls of animals, too, from the dog to the camel, from the griffin to the horse, from the stork to the turtle, are immortal like those of man.

> If one alone is the genus of beings constituted by a body and soul, the type that we call animal, because in it all the animals subsist in a substantial way—in fact, man and lion, ox and horse are in it only one thing and only one substance (*in ipso unum sunt et substuntiale unum*)—how can all the species that belong to this genus perish, and only the human species remain? [...] If all the species are one thing alone in genus (*in genere unum*), how can that one thing perish in one part and remain in another? (737C–738A)

Realizing the scandalous character of his affirmation, he prudently seeks to temper its radicality:

> Let no one believe that we say this to destroy the argumentation of the holy fathers, but rather as a way of seeking within the limits of our strength what must be held as valid from them [...]. We maintain such things without prejudicing anyone's interpretations, instead persuading readers to investigate more attentively and to follow what will seem most probable to them after having consulted the truth (739B).

3.3. After having treated in the first book the nature non-created and creating, namely, God as cause of all things, in the second book the nature created and creating, namely, the primordial causes, and in the third book the nature created and not creating, namely, the things generated in space and time, Eriugena dedicates the fourth book of the *Periphyseon* to the 'return of all things in the nature that does not create nor is it created', that is, to nature in the final and first condition of absolute immanence to itself, when the process that led God to go out from himself into creation has arrived at its eternal completion. Here the ship of the mind, which in the preceding books had traversed 'a still sea without risk of shipwreck because of the tranquillity of its waves', must instead contend with 'impervious waters full of tortuous ravines [. . .] where it is easy to make shipwreck due to the fogginess of the most subtle interpretations, which are like hidden crags that break ships' (743D).

Indeed, it is a matter of a rereading of the Genesis narrative on the creation of man and his dwelling in the earthly paradise in order to understand its ultimate meaning, which, contrary to Augustine's *ad litteram*, can only be allegorical. The compass that allows the author to remain happily on course is, once again, the unconditioned unity of nature (life) and soul, of physiology and psychology. 'There is in fact,' he writes,

> a most general and common nature of all things, created by one sole principle of everything, and from it, as from a great spring, there gush forth, through the hidden passages of the bodily creature, the streams of the diverse forms of singular things. This potential that comes forth through diverse seeds from the secrets of nature bursts forth first of all in the seed itself, then is mixed with diverse humors and finally ferments into the singular things (750A).

The genus of all living beings is therefore one, and humanity, according to a theorem that Eriugena never stops repeating, 'was created in the universal genus of animals' (*in universali animalium genere homo conditus est*) (751A).

The theorem is all the more risky, because it calls into question the privileged status of humanity with respect to living beings. If man was created in the one genus of animals, if he is completely animal like other living beings— asks the *Alumnus*, the interlocutor from whom Eriugena has the most pressing objections arise, at this point—'how is it possible that only man and no other animal was created in the image of God?' (750C). The *Nutritor's* response is a masterwork of subtlety, which, while apparently maintaining the primacy of humanity, in reality ends up cancelling it. God created man in the genus of animals, because he wanted to create all of nature in him (764B). The superiority of humanity rests only on the fact that all living beings, from fish to reptiles to birds, are in him, as humanity is in them: 'Do you not see that humanity is in all the animals and all the animals are in humanity and man is above all the animals?' (752C).

For this reason, with a masterly use of contradiction, Eriugena affirms that 'one can rightly say that "man is an animal" (*homo animal est*) and "man is not an animal" (*homo animal non est*).' To the radicality of the first thesis, which derives necessarily from the inseparable unity of life, are counterposed, to motivate the second, commonplaces of the ecclesiastical tradition: 'In its most elevated part, reason, the intellect, and the internal sense, he surpasses all that is comprised in the nature of the animals' (753A).

But to the question of the *Alumnus* that asks whether this means that there two souls in man, one animal and the other created in the image of God, the *Nutritor* responds unreservedly (*firmissime teneo*) that the human soul is one and indivisible:

It is completely the same everywhere (*tota enim in se ipsa ubique est*). It is completely life, completely intellect, completely reason, completely sense, completely memory, completely vivifies the body, nourishes it, maintains it, causes it to grow (*tota siquidem vita est, tota intellectus, tota ratio, tota sensus, tota memoria, tota corpus vivificat, nutrit, continet, auget*) (754C).

Hence, while remaining one, it can be called by many names, according to the number of its movements:

While it moves within the divine essence, it is called mind, soul, and intellect; in the moment when it considers the natures and causes of created things, it is called reason; when it welcomes by means of the bodily senses the forms of sensible beings, it is called sensation; when it carries out in the body its secret movements according to its similarity to rational animals, nourishing it and causing it to grow, it is customarily called life; but in all these movements it is everywhere whole (754D).

At this point Eriugena can discretely leave to the *Alumnus* the task of pronouncing the thesis that annuls every difference in humanity between the animal and the divine: 'Thus the soul was all produced from the earth in the genus of the animals and all created in the image of God (*Tota igitur et in genere animalium de terra producta est et tota ad imaginem Dei facta*)' (ibid.). A few lines later the *Nutritor* makes it explicit in the theorem that most fully summarizes the novelty of Eriugena's thought:

> Do not be disturbed, therefore, about what we have said about human nature, that it is completely itself everywhere: entirely image of God in the animal and entirely animal in the image of God (*imaginem in animali tota et animal in imagine totum*). Everything that its creator primordially created in it remains integral in its totality (*totum integrum manet*) (761B).

And it is significant that to the question of the *Alumnus* which asks him why God wanted to create only man and not the other creatures in his image, the *Nutritor* can only respond: 'I admit that I am completely ignorant of that (*fateor me omnino ignorare*)' (764B).

3.4. It is by starting from the firm position of these premises that Eriugena can proceed to his very original interpretation of the earthly paradise and of sin. Against Augustine, who knows only one creation and 'affirms in all his books that the body of the first man before sin was and remained an animal and earthly body' (803B), Eriugena, invoking the authority of Gregory, seems to break creation, in itself unitary, down into two moments. The body that was created in the first creation was spiritual and immortal, 'similar to that which we will have in the resurrection' (800A); the corruptible and mortal body was added to the first in a second creation as a consequence of sin. Nevertheless—and here lies the subtlety of his doctrine— since in God 'there is not past or future or a middle between them, because all things are contemporaneous for him (*ipsi omnia simul sunt*)' (808B), to speak of a before and after sin has meaning only for the mutability of our thoughts, subjected to temporal categories. What really happened is that

> God, even before man sinned, created in man and together with man the consequences of sin, in such a way that, among the qualities created in man, some are considered the work of the divine goodness [. . .] others, by contrast, the work of a crime known in advance (807C).

The consequences of sin—an animal, earthly and corruptible body, the modality of procreation similar to the beasts, the need for food and drink, etc.—did not happen, as in the Augustinian paradigm, as punishment of a sin that at a certain point contaminated human nature. They were created, with a sort of sublime irony, by the divine wisdom before any sinful event whatsoever, as an animal body that was added to the first not as a second body, but as a mutable and corruptible clothing that always already clothes the spiritual body.

> The body is in fact one, which, united in a connatural and substantial way to the soul, makes up the human being (803A).

Let us reflect on the implications of this singular doctrine. If the consequences of sin were created by God before it, as part of a single human nature that, even in its animality, is entirely in the image of God, then the very possibility of an original sin in Augustine's sense is destroyed from its foundations. Following his usual strategy, the *Nutritor* here cites Augustine to make him anticipate the corollaries that Eriugena intends to draw from his own theorems. If Augustine, in *De civitate Dei* (14.26) wrote that 'man would live (*vivebat*) in paradise' and not 'lived' (*vixit*) or 'had lived (*vixerat*) in paradise',[1] this is because he is using the verb in an inchoative sense,

> as if he had said openly 'he was beginning to live in paradise' [...] In fact this kind of past tense is called inchoative by those who attentively examine the meaning of verbal tenses: it indicates the beginning or the auspices of something that is not in any way complete (808D–809A).

The unheard-of thesis that Eriugena proposes at this point is that man actually never dwelled in paradise. Adam's life in paradise is to be understood, according to the inchoative meaning of the verb, as it if referred to the future and not to a past. Just as Augustine—invoked once again to prove a doctrine contrary to his own—wrote in his commentary on Genesis that the devil had never been blessed among the angels, but fell from the very beginning

---

1 The three Latin verbs are in the imperfect, perfect and pluperfect tenses, respectively. As Eriugena claims, the Latin imperfect can indeed refer to an action that is just beginning or even intended, though it is used more often for open-ended past actions. My translation of 'would live' is an attempt to capture a similar double meaning in English, albeit by bridging a somewhat antiquated usage ('would' in the sense of 'wanted to' or 'intended to') and a more colloquial one (as in phrases like 'When I was young, we would always go to the park to play', indicating habitual actions in the past). [Trans.]

of his creation, so nothing prevents us from thinking that 'man, without any temporal interval, without any sensible act, was not in the paradise in which he had been naturally created, but immediately swerved from the way of truth (*mox de via veritatis deviasse*)' (812B). All the things that Holy Scripture narrates as if they happened in paradise 'are to be understood as happening outside paradise and after sin (*extra paradisum et post peccatum fuisse intelligenda*)' (833C).

The fact is—here Eriugena shows his cards—that paradise, as Origen and Ambrose had already suggested, is not a real, earthly, wooded place, but is to be understood allegorically as human nature itself:

> With the word 'paradise', divine scripture has expressed in a figurative way the human nature made in the image of God. The true plantation of God is this nature that he created in Eden in the image and likeness of himself [. . .]. The fertile land of this plantation was a potentially immortal body [. . .]. And the water of this land capable of all forms was the sensitive faculty of an incorruptible body (822A).

But if this is so, if the Garden is only human nature, then man has never entered into his nature or has always already exited from it. That man has not yet even entered into paradise, that what scripture narrates about sin and the fall should be understood as having happened outside paradise, this means that sin happened outside human nature, that human nature was never contaminated by it: 'If paradise is the plantation of God in delights,' affirms the *Nutritor*, 'the human nature created in the image of God was not deformed by any contact with sin' (837A).

It is difficult to imagine a more extreme Pelagianism, which denies at its root the Augustinian doctrine of the nature corrupted and *facta peccatrix* (made sinful) once and for all by Adam's sin.

> Just as the divine goodness is entirely in all the creatures that participate in it and there is no wickedness or stupidity or ignorance that can impede it from penetrating the totality of what is created, so too human nature (*humanitas*) is diffused in all human beings and is all in all, good or bad though they be. It is not repelled by the stupidity of anyone nor held back by anyone's wickedness; it is not corrupted by vice or polluted by anyone's filthiness. Pure in all, it is not inflated in the proud or shrivelled in the cowardly, it is no larger in larger bodies or smaller in smaller ones, but,

equally in all, it reaches the same point in those who participate in it; it is not better in the good than it is in the wicked, it is not worse in the wicked than it is in the good, it is not more integral in intact bodies than it is in those who, for whatever reason, lose their integrity or do not reach it (942C).

This incorruptibility of human nature with respect to sin extends, with an obvious revival of themes from Origen, to the punishment that the tradition assigns to sin. 'Human nature, just as it is free and completely released from all sin, is also universally free and released from all punishment of sin' (943C).

While the judges of secular trials punish the whole body together with the crime, God punishes 'in an ineffable way' the crime and not the nature. In any case, 'both in the just and in the impious, human nature is always saved, intact, and not contaminated' (946A).

3.5. The human nature created in the animal genus in the image of God (that is, paradise) is—such is the ultimate meaning of Eriugena's thesis—always already present in its entirety, and yet man has not yet entered into it or has always already exited from it. What is called sin is this exit, which in reality precedes every sinful act. Commenting on Luke 10:30, 'A man was going down from Jerusalem to Jericho and ran into robbers,' Eriugena reads it as an allegory for the exit of man from paradise, that is, from his nature:

> It does not in fact say: 'A man was in Jerusalem and ran into robbers.' If human nature had remained in Jerusalem (namely, in paradise), it certainly would not have encountered the robbers (that is, the devil with his followers). [. . .] In this passage it is to be understood that man fell in himself before being tempted by the devil. Not only is this to be understood, but also that not in paradise, but exiting from it (*descendente eo*) and while he was abandoning by his own will the happiness of paradise (the word Jerusalem means the vision of peace) and was sliding towards Jericho (that is, into this world), it was injured by the devil and robbed (811C).

There is not a sin that could corrupt human nature, because man is always already *descendens*, in exit from it. Evil is this 'descent' and, as such, it cannot have any natural cause. The sole cause of evil is the will:

Sins are not natural but voluntary (*non enim peccata naturalia sunt, sed voluntaria*). The cause of all sin, in the angel as in man, is one's own perverse will (*propria perversaque voluntas*). But the cause of this perverse will is not found in the natural movements of the rational creature. The good cannot indeed be cause of evil and this latter is, for this reason, deprived of cause and lacking in every natural origin (944A).

With an intuition that anticipates Spinoza's doctrine, evil, 'which does not subsist in the nature of things', is defined by Eriugena not as a substance, but as 'a defect of potential (*intimae virtutis defectus*)' (ibid.). It does not consist in anything other than an abuse of the goods contained in human nature (*praeter naturalibus bonis abusionem*) (975B). What can be punished is, therefore, the movement of the will, not that of nature, which

> subsists in itself everywhere and in all those that participate in it through a good, safe, whole, uninjured, uncontaminated, incorruptible, impassible and immutable participation in the highest good, everywhere blessed, glorious in the elect, in whom it is deified, excellent in the reprobate, who are

contained in it so that their substantial property
may not be reduced to nothing (944B).

3.6. Let us consider the singular status that Eriugena
assigns to the earthly paradise. Insofar as it coincides with
human nature, it exists from all time, even if not necessarily in the form of an earthly place, and it will never cease
to exist. And man—which is to say, the living being that
still does not have access to its own nature, because, by
abusing its goods, it has always already abandoned it—will
necessarily end up returning to it, when all things will be
restored to their cause. Paradise—human nature—is that
to which man must return without ever truly having been
there. On the other hand, the return is not to be understood in a temporal sense, but has always already taken
place, in such a way that exit and return are co-present. It
is not surprising at this point that, already in the second
book of the *Periphyseon*, Eriugena had been able to formu-
late the bold thesis, which the humanists would take up
again only in the sixteenth century, according to which
paradise is not actually different from the earth, because
in the primordial causes their foundation is one and the
same: 'Paradise,' he writes,

is not distinguished from this earthly habitable world by volume or spaces, but only by the diversity of the mode of sojourning there and the difference of beatitude. Even the first man, in fact, if he had not sinned, would have been able to live happily on earth, because one and the same is, in the primordial causes, the foundation of the earth and that of paradise (538B).

For this reason, 'in paradise, as in an immense and most happy temple, all men will enter, each according to his own propotion' (928B). And this temple—human nature and the earth—in which man always already is, but has never yet entered, is also the place in which God dwells: 'Indeed, God does not dwell elsewhere than in the human nature and in the angelic nature, and only to these is given the contemplation of truth' (ibid.).

It is striking that theological reflection on human nature coincides to such a degree with that on the meaning of the earthly paradise and on the reality of the originary transgression, that it can be said that the very concept of 'human nature' is elaborated by theologians in close relation to the notion of sin and draws from the latter its constitutive ambiguity. In the Augustinian tradition, which wound up prevailing in the Latin Church, nature and sin are indissolubly linked and human nature is irrevocably split into an originary nature, now lost, and a *natura lapsa.* Paradise is, consequently, a real historical place, where man was placed by God, but from which he exited forever when sin contaminated his nature. It is now, exactly like the prelapsarian nature, forever inaccessible, and the cherubim with the flaming sword keeps watch so that man does not seek to penetrate it undeservedly. The only possibility of restoring in some measure the original nature, which is incurably corrupted, is consigned to a history and an economy of salvation—in which the Church works through the sacraments—and to another paradise, the heavenly one, which does not coincide with the first and is reserved only—in the future and never in the present—to the elect. The *natura lapsa* continues and will continue to exist in hell, where it eternally suffers its penalty.

In the second model, which is that of Eriugena, paradise—that is, human nature—is completely alien to sin and the history of the fall narrated by Genesis must be understood to have happened outside of it. There is not properly a history of salvation, because human nature is always already saved. Paradise—life in all its forms—was never lost: it is always in its place and remains as an untouched model of the good even in the continual abuse that man makes of it, without managing in any case to corrupt it. The heavenly paradise, which is not distinguished from the earthly one, into which man has not yet penetrated, coincides with the return to the originary nature that, untouched and pure, awaits all humanity from the beginning of time.

4

The Divine Forest

4.1. That the earthly paradise and the encounter with
Matelda have a central function in the *Divine Comedy* has
already been observed. It is here, writes Giovanni Pascoli,
in the 'wonderful vision' of the Garden, that

> Dante *found himself*, found his Matelda, his art, his
> poem: his poem, which goes from a wood to a for-
> est and from the forest to the empyrean; his poem,
> of which the center is that forest where Matelda
> is, who in herself unites the active and contempla-
> tive life [. . .] (2000: 539).

Precisely in the case of this decisive episode, however, in
which poetic and theologico-philosophical motifs are so
tightly interwoven, the exegetes have shown themselves to

be, with few exceptions, especially insufficient. As concerns Matelda, who is surely by all evidence a poetic invention, it has been almost exclusively a question, following the dominant canon of gossip, of identifying a real person with the same name—be it, without any apparent reason, the countess Matilda of Canossa or, equally without motive, the Benedictine nuns Matilda of Hackenborn and Mechthild of Magdeburg or, finally, simply 'a pretty Florentine woman'. Moreover, in this case as well, Dante's ideas are constantly traced back to those of contemporary theologians—in particular Aquinas. Even one of the most acute interpreters, Charles Singleton, who has dedicated to the episode of the earthly paradise and to the figure of Matelda a book that is certainly useful, takes care to specify that Dante does not invent his theories but accepts them, 'as notions already existing in the thought and doctrine of his day' (1958: 16). As if the mind of Dante (who after all often took care to define himself explicitly as a philosopher) were not, for originality, inventive capacity, and coherence, infinitely superior to that of the scholastic philosophers who were his contemporaries, Aquinas included; and as if *inventio* were not an integral part of poetic practice, which would otherwise be reduced to the futile task of dressing up in rhetorical expedients ideas found by others.

This originality and inventive capacity finds testimony above all in his description of the 'ancient forest' of the earthly paradise, which, if it shares some aspects with traditional representations, departs from them to such a degree that one can say that the image that results is decisively new, if not heretical. Not only have the four rivers from Genesis 2:10–14, the Pichon, Gihon, Tigris and Euphrates, which are an essential part of all the descriptions, disappeared, replaced by two others, which are now called Lethe and Eunoe and which carry out an important function in Dante's itinerary towards innocence; not only do there shine on Eden four stars (which are also nymphs), of which Genesis makes no mention, but—and this is truly unheard-of—the garden, which, according to a constant tradition, must be empty or in which only Elijah and Enoch have found a provisional dwelling, is inhabited by a woman in love who sings and dances: 'A lady all alone, who went singing and culling flower from flower with which all her way was painted' (*Una donna soletta che si gia / cantando e scegliendo fior da fiore / ond' era pinta tutta la sua via*) (*Purgatorio* 28.40–2), 'singing like a lady enamoured' (*cantando come donna innamorata*) (ibid. 29.1). The encounter with this maiden is described as an amorous encounter, not only because from her eyes sparkles the same light that shines 'beneath the lids' (*sotto le ciglia*) of Venus when she has been shot by the arrow of Eros (ibid. 28.64–6), but because Dante too seems kindled by the same love, if he can compare himself to Leander enamoured with Hero (ibid. 28.73–5). The whole scene recalls, as has been suggested, the lyric genre of the 'pastoral', in which the poet, wandering through the fields, describes his encounter with a maiden in love. The suggestion is all the more convincing in that the description of the woman in Paradise ('*una donna soletta che si gia*', '*cantando come donna innamorata*') seem to intentionally evoke the corresponding verses in Guido Cavalcanti's 'pastoral' *In un boschetto trova' pasturella*, which Dante could not have been unfamiliar with: '*che sola sola per lo bosco gia*', '*cantava come fosse 'nnamotara*'.

If this does not mean that one should see in Matelda an allegory of courtly love, it is certain, nevertheless, that she has so much to do with the universe of amorous lyric that some have been able to speak appropriately of an 'underlying Stilnovism of this episode'. On condition of not forgetting, however, that—as Dante never stops repeating in the *Convivio*—love, which the Intelligences that move the heaven of Venus breathe onto 'souls here below' (*Convivio* 2.5.13), is inseparable from philosophy and from the happiness that derives from it, of which it is so to speak the form (*amore è forma di Filosofia*) (ibid. 3.13.10).

4.2. It will then be a good rule, suspending at least for the moment every interpretive hypothesis, for us to stick to what Dante himself directly or indirectly tells us. It is in fact the case that he pronounces beyond any possible doubt what is for him the meaning of the earthly paradise. I am thinking of the passage from *De monarchia* (3.16.4) in which, expounding the doctrine of the two beatitudes that constitutes one of the cornerstones of his thought, he writes:

> *Duos igitur fines Providentia illa inenarrabilis homini proposuit intendendos: beatitudinem scilicet huius vite, que in operatione proprie virtutis consistit et per terrestrem paradisum figuratur; et beatitudinem vite eterne, que consistit in fruitione divini aspectus ad quam propria virtus ascendere non potest, nisi lumine divino adiuta, que per paradisum celeste intelligi datur.* (Ineffable Providence has assigned to man two ends to which he tends: namely, the beatitude of this life, which consists in the operation of his own virtue and is prefigured by the earthly Paradise; and the beatitude of life

everlasting, which consists in the enjoyment of the
vision of God, to which man's natural powers may
not attain unless aided by divine illumination, and
which may be understood by means of the celestial Paradise.)

The earthly paradise is therefore a figure or an allegory of
the beatitude of human nature that Dante elsewhere calls,
based on one of its parts, 'civil' ('human nature has not
only one beatitude but two, namely that of the civil life
and that of the contemplative life' [*Convivio* 2.4.10]). The
qualification 'civil' is important, because it implies that—
despite the silence of interpreters in this connection—the
episode of the earthly paradise does not relate only to the
life of the individual by the name of Dante, but also has
an immediately political meaning, which concerns the
human race in its entirety (the *humana civilitas* of *De
Monarchia* [1.3.1]).

Since the two levels—individual and collective—are
tightly interwoven, I will attempt to examine them without
ever forgetting their parallelism. An initial observation,
insofar as it concerns the itinerary of the man Dante,
is that a minimally attentive reading reveals a striking
correspondence between the 'dark wood' (*selva oscura*), in
which the poet has got lost at the beginning of the poem,

and the 'ancient wood' (*selva antica*) of the Garden. Not only is the forest of paradise no less dark than the first ('under the perpetual shade which never lets sun or moon shine there'; *sotto l'ombra perpetua, che mai / raggiar non lascia sole ivi né luna* [*Purgatorio* 28.32–3]), but the poet, having just entered the wood, seems to discretely cite the *Inferno*: 'that I could not see the place where I had entered' (*ch'io non potea rivedere ond'io mi 'ntrassi*) (*Purgatorio* 28.23–4), 'I cannot rightly tell how I entered there' (*Io non so ben ridir com'i v'intrai* [*Inferno* 1.10]—one should note the analogy: *rivedere/ridire*; significantly, both verbs refer to something already seen and already said). The sleep that burdens the mind of the poet at the entrance of the dark wood ('I was so full of sleep at that moment'; *tant'era pieno di sonno a quel punto* [ibid. 1.11]) returns to surprise the poet on the threshold of the earthly paradise, even if this time the drowsiness presages omens ('sleep seized me; sleep, which often has news before the event'; *mi prese il sonno; il sonno che sovente, anzi che 'l fatto sia, sa le novelle* [*Purgatorio* 27.92–3]). Even where he is concerned to draw a contrast, the symmetry in the triple adjectives ('The divine forest thick and lively'; *La divina foresta spessa e viva* [*Purgatorio* 28.2]; 'that wood, savage and harsh and dense'; *esta selva selvaggia e aspra e forte* [*Inferno* 1.5]) emphasizes a correspondence that must not be missed.

It is as if Dante wants to suggest to us that the two woods are in reality one sole forest, one time as a place of bitterness and death (*Tant'è amara che poco è più morte*) and another as a place of sweetness and life (*l'aura dolce; spessa e viva*). The wood in which the poet has got lost at the beginning of the poem is, namely, the same Garden in which he will have to find himself again. And if the earthly paradise is, as we know, only a figure of the 'beatitude of this life', this means that the man Dante—and with him all humanity—has been lost in that felicity that was assigned to him as end of his earthly life. Thus does Virgil's admonishment on the threshold of paradise gain its full meaning: 'Take henceforth thy pleasure for guide' (*lo tu piacere omai prendi per duce*) (*Purgatorio* 27.131): now that his intelligence has been restored to its original rectitude ('Free, upright and whole is your will'; *libero, dritto e sano è tuo arbitrio* [ibid. 27.140]), what will guide Dante is the same pleasure in which he had got lost at the beginning. And if intellect and love are for him indistinguishable, then Dante as poet has been lost in the same amorous beatitude that was the material of his rhymes (this suffices to demonstrate the 'underlying Stilnovism' that scholars have found in the description of the Garden). And just as he was lost in it, in it—that is, in the earthly paradise of which it is the figure—he will have to find himself again.

4.3. The text cited from *De monarchia* clearly pronounces what beatitude consists in, taking up an Aristotelian definition: in the exercise of one's virtue (*in operatione proprie virtutis*). How this operation can be actualized and how it is intimately tied to love is specified in a passage from the *Convivio* (4.21-2) while 'discussing human felicity and its sweetness'. Dante develops there a theory of the 'natural appetite', which 'the Greeks call *hormen*' and which 'sprouts from divine grace'; as in Eriugena, it does not differ in origin from 'that which comes simply [*nudamente*] from nature', namely, the vital impulse that leads all living beings to love themselves, but later, 'as this appetite proceeds', it orients its love toward the better part of itself, namely, the soul and reason:

> Therefore if the mind always delights in the use of the thing that is loved, which is the fruit of love, and if in that thing which is loved most of all is found the most delightful use of all, the use of our mind is most of all delightful to us. And whatever is most of all delightful to us constitutes our happiness and our beatitude [. . .] (ibid. 4.22.9)

The exercise of one's own virtue, in which there consists the felicity of which the earthly paradise is a figure, coincides with the 'use of the thing that is loved'—it is, that is to say, essentially an act of love. For this reason, the person whom Dante encounters in the earthly paradise is a woman in love; for this reason, Matelda, who is the cipher of Edenic felicity, has to do with love. And the poet must newly traverse in the 'divine forest' that amorous experience in whose 'dark wood' he had been lost at the beginning.

4.4. Dante does not limit himself to indicating to us that the earthly paradise is the figure of earthly beatitude. Through the mouth of Matelda, he institutes a striking correspondence between the Garden in Genesis and the golden age sung by pagan poets. According to the 'corollary' that the enamoured woman adds to her commentary on the geography of paradise, 'Those who in old times sang of the age of gold and of its happy state perhaps dreamed on Parnassus of this place' (*quelli ch' anticamente poetaro / l'età de l'oro e suo stato felice, / forse in Parnaso esto loco sognaro*') (*Purgatorio* 28.139–41). The correspondence is all the more significant insofar as Dante had evoked the golden age a little earlier, which Virgil in *Eclogue* 4 calls *Saturnia regna* and of which he prophetically announces the return. Indeed, Dante puts in the mouth of Statius the Virgilian verses in question, translated almost literally: 'When you said: "The age turns new again; justice comes back and the primal years of men, and a new race descends from heaven'" (*quando dicesti: 'Secol si rinova; / torna giustizia e primo tempo umano, / e progenie scende da ciel nova'*) (ibid. 22.70–2). No less significant is the fact that in his political treatise, probably composed in the same years as the *Comedy*, Dante evokes the golden age (*optima tempora, quae etiam aurea nuncupabant*) in connection with justice, again citing the verses from the *Eclogue*:

> Further, the world is disposed for the best when justice reigns therein most powerfully. For this reason, Virgil, desiring to glorify that age which seemed to be dawning in his own day, sang in his *Eclogues, Iam redit et virgo, redeunt Saturnia regna* ('Now doth the Virgin return and the kingdoms of Saturn'). For they called justice the 'virgin', whom they also called Astraea; and they called 'kingdoms of Saturn' the best times, which they also said were golden (*De Monarchia* 1.11.1).

If we must take this correspondence seriously—and I do not see why we should not do so—this means that, for Dante, the earthly paradise, as figure of earthly beatitude, was also the place of the original justice of human nature, which the ancients conceived as a maiden (*virgo*) by the name of Astrea. This has led Singleton to see in Matelda a personification of original justice, which is certainly possible (all the more so in that Dante compares her expressly to a 'virgin' [*Purgatorio* 28.57]), on condition that we do not forget, however, that we are dealing with a complex creation, to whom Dante seems to consign, as he does after all to Beatrice, an extraordinary figural richness. In any case, the possible meanings of this figure are intrinsically connected: earthly beatitude, the amorous use in which it is translated, the natural justice that belongs to the 'human root'.

4.5. The evocation of the 'virgin' and the golden age in *De monarchia* suggests that Matelda and the earthly paradise have, as it was legitimate to expect, a political meaning as well. At the beginning of the treatise, in fact, Dante asks what is the end of the human race and, consistently with what we already know, he identifies it in a 'certain proper operation of human universality' (*aliqua propria operatio humane universitatis*) (1.3.4). And since what defines human nature is not to be simply animate, as plants also are, not to be capable of learning, because so are animals as well, nor to be always intelligent in action, as are angels, but, rather, to be capable of understanding by means of the possible intellect (which is to say, to have the potential or possibility of thinking: *esse apprehensivum per intellectum possibilem* [ibid. 1.3.6]) then the proper operation of the human race will be that of always actualizing all the potential of the possible intellect (*proprium opus humani generis totaliter accepti est actuare semper totam potentiam intellectus possibilis*) (ibid. 1.4.1).

Dante here takes up an Averroistic theme in order to deduce from it the necessity of universal monarchy, since the potential of the possible intellect cannot be actuated by one man alone nor by one city alone, but demands the *multitudo* of the race ('since this potential cannot be entirely reduced to action simultaneously by one man alone, or through any one of the particular communities, it is necessary that there be in the human race a multitude, through which this entire potential may be actualized [*necesse est multitudinem esse in humano genere, per quam quidem tota potentia hec actuetur*]' [ibid. 1.3.8]). And since the realization of the end of the human race coincides with felicity, one can understand why the treatise, immediately before concluding, mentions, as we have seen, the earthly paradise as figure of the 'beatitude of this life'.

The theme of the possible intellect had already been evoked—even if not in its political meaning—in the *Convivio* (and later taken up in the discourse of Statius in

Purgatorio 25). Asking how 'goodness' descends into the human nature, Dante here espouses a true and proper doctrine of the formation of the foetus and of the 'generative soul', which unites what we would define as an embryology *in nuce* with philosophical and theological motifs: 'Therefore I say,' he writes,

> that when the human seed falls into its receptacle, namely, its matrix, it carries with it the virtue of the generative soul, and the virtue of heaven and the virtue of the combined elements, namely temperament. It matures and disposes the material to the formative virtue given by the soul of the generator, and the formative virtue prepares the organs to receive the celestial virtue, which brings the soul from the potentiality of the seed into life (*Convivio* 4.21.4).

It is at this point that Dante, while distancing himself from Averroes, introduces the decisive function fo the possible or material intellect, which in the history of thought has remained linked to Aristotle's commentator par excellence, whom he will have encountered in the 'philosophical family' of the first circle: 'As it is produced it receives from the virtue of the celestial mover the possible intellect,

which draws all the universal forms into itself potentially'
(ibid. 4.21.5).

The proper operation, in the exercise of which consists
the felicity of both the singular human and the human
race, coincides with the actualization of this intellective
potential, in which, as the canzone 'Amor che ne la mente
mi ragiona' takes care to specify, love 'makes its operation'
(in accordance with Cavalcanti, who, in his doctrinal masterwork, had situated the origin of life there: 'It comes
from visible form that takes on, and embraces—in possible
intellect, as in the subject—location and dwelling'; *'ven da
veduta forma che s'intende / che prende nel possibile intelletto / come
in subietto, loco e dimoranza*' [Cavalcanti, 'Donna me prega,
—per ch'eo voglio dire']). It will not be impertinent, then,
to add to the figural meanings of Matelda (which are the
varied faces of a single truth) also that of being a personification of the possible intellect, in its double meaning,
both collective and individual.

4.6. Let us now attempt to define Dante's earthly paradise
with respect to the theological tradition and, in particular,
the doctrine of original sin. The Garden is certainly also
for Dante a place on earth, situated on the top of a very

high mountain in the southern hemisphere; but, as we have seen, it differs decisively from the paradise described in Genesis. Above all it is not uninhabited and contains, moreover, two rivers that not only do not correspond to the four named in sacred Scripture, but, on closer inspection, are completely incompatible with the earthly paradise that they describe. The first, in particular, which, significantly, is called Lethe, 'removes all memory of sin', which is doubly impossible, if it is truly to be found in the paradise of Genesis: once, because in this way the Garden would have already contained in itself the expectation of sin, and a second time because Adam and Eve would have then been able, as does Dante, to immerse themselves in it and forget their guilt. Although commentators do not seem to have noted this obvious contradiction, we must conclude from it that the river described by Matelda has been introduced into paradise in a second moment, replacing those from Genesis. It lacks, moreover—and this is particularly significant—any indication of the cherubim with the flaming sword who guards the way into the Garden. Dante—who represents humanity—can enter it without any impediment.

The paradise in which Dante encounters Matelda has thus undergone a transformation with respect to that in which Adam found himself; it is and is not the same 'ancient wood' from which the progenitors were driven out. By entering into the Garden, Dante enters now—in the present—into a primordial past, which—as happens in memory—has for this reason necessarily changed. This temporal dislocation allow us to explain the peremptory use of the present on Beatrice's part ('Did you not know that here man *is* happy?'; *non sapei tu che qui è l'uom felice?* [*Purgatorio* 30.75]), which contrasts with Matelda's 'was' ('here the human root was innocent'; *qui fu innocente l'umana radice* [ibid. 28.142]); man, who was innocent in Adam's paradise, is still happy in Matelda's garden.

4.7. At this point reconstructing the fundamental outlines of Dante's doctrine on original sin becomes unavoidable. Shortly before Dante's entry into the earthly paradise, Marco Lombardo makes an affirmation that unequivocally denies the Augustinian doctrine, of which it takes up the terms in order to negate them: 'You can see plainly that ill-guiding is the cause that has made the world wicked, and not nature that is corrupt in you' (*Ben puoi veder che la mala condotta / è la cagion che 'l mondo ha fatto reo / e non natura che 'n voi sia corrotta*) (ibid. 16.103–05). We are dealing with an openly Pelagian thesis, which almost literally retraces the ideas that Augustine attributes to Pelagius: there are some, Pelagius is supposed to have said according to Augustine, 'who, while they should accuse human will for their own sins, seek to excuse themselves by instead accusing human nature' (*De natura et gratia* 1.1).

How to reconcile this clear thesis with the orthodox doctrine that Beatrice seems to repeat in *Paradiso* (7.85–7): 'Your nature, when it all sinned in its seed, was parted from these dignities, as from paradise' (*Vostra natura, quando peccò tota / nel seme suo, da queste dignitadi, / come di paradiso, fu remota*)? An attentive reading of the following verses shows that the contradiction is only apparent. Beatrice there lays out, in fact, a theory of redemption that, in distinction from Augustine's, attributes to the incarnation of the Son a complete restitution of human nature in its original dignity. There were, affirms Beatrice, two ways to repair the sin of the protoplasts: 'either that God, of his own sole clemency, had pardoned, or that man, of himself, had given satisfaction for his folly' (*o che Dio solo per sua cortesia / dimesso avesse, o che l'om per se isso / avesse soddisfatto a sua follia*) (ibid. 7.91–3). God chose to use both ways: through the incarnation, in fact, he involved human nature in some way in the work of redemption: 'For God was more bounteous in giving himself so as to make man sufficient to raise himself again than if, simply of himself, he had pardoned' (*ché più largo fu Dio a dar se stesso / per far l'uom sufficiente a rilevarsi, / che s'elli avesse sol da sé dimesso*) (ibid. 7.115–17). In *Monarchia* (2.11.2), the thesis is solidly confirmed: 'If for that sin (of Adam), satisfaction had not been given with the death of Christ, we would still be sons of wrath by nature, that is, by the corrupt nature (*adhuc essemus filii ire natura, natura scilicet depravata*).'

This is an absolutely original theological doctrine, according to which the becoming human of God has rendered human nature 'sufficient to lift himself up again' (*sufficiente a rilevarsi*), in such a way that it is fully reintegrated in its original condition ('to restore man to his full life'; *riparare l'omo a sua intera vita* [*Paradiso* 7.104]). To gauge the novelty of this position, one must not forget that the expression 'sufficient to lift himself up again' not only contradicts Augustine's thesis, restated many times, according to which anyone who maintains that 'the human will is sufficient (*sufficere voluntatem*) not to sin [. . .] must be anathemized (*anathemandum esse*)' (*De perfectione iustitiae hominis* 21.44), because redemption has not completely liberated human nature from its corruption; but, according to Aquinas' doctrine as well, the sacraments are necessary after the coming of Christ, on account of the condition in which man finds himself after sin:

> Since by sinning man subjected himself by his affections to corporeal things, it is necessary to apply the medicine to man in the same place that has been affected by disease. Consequently, it was fitting that God make use of corporeal signs to administer to man a spiritual medicine (*Summa Theologica* 3a, q. 61, a. 1, co.).

There is nothing of this in Dante: for him, the incarnation of Christ is perfectly sufficient for the cancellation of sin and his position with respect to the sacraments—which he never mentions in the *Comedy*, except with reference to the corruption of the Church—is instead comparable to that of those—whom Aquinas takes care to contradict—who affirm that 'there was no need for any sacraments after Christ came. For the figure should cease with the advent of the truth [. . .]. Since, therefore, the sacraments are signs or figures of the truth, it seems that there was no need for any sacraments after Christ's Passion' (ibid. 3a, q. 61, a. 4, arg. 1). It is not surprising, then, that in the *Convivio* he can interpret the 'song of the Prophet which says that when the people of Israel went out of Egypt, Judea was made whole and free' in the sense that 'when the soul

departs from sin it is made whole and free in its power'
(2.1.6–7); nor that Virgil can take leave of Dante at the
threshold of the earthly paradise with the unequivocal
assertion: 'Free, upright, and whole is your will' (*libero, dritto
e sano è tuo arbitrio*) (*Purgatorio* 27.140). It is this freedom
that—in a passage from *De Monarchia* in which Pelagian
echoes sound—is claimed as the 'greatest gift of God to
human nature':

> One must know that the first principle of our
> freedom is freedom of the will (*libertas arbitrii*),
> which many have on their lips, but few in their
> heart [. . .]. If judgement is moved in some way
> by appetite (as would happen if human nature
> were irredeemably corrupted), it would not be free
> [. . .]. It is obvious, therefore, that this freedom
> of this principle of all our freedom is the greatest
> gift extended by God to human nature, as I have
> said in the *Paradiso* of the *Comedy* (*sicut in Paradiso
> Comedie iam dixit*), since through it we are happy
> here as men and elsewhere we will be happy
> through it as gods (1.12.2–6).

Freedom and happiness are indissolubly connected in
human nature—in origin and, thanks to the incarnation of Christ, even now. The 'divine forest' of paradise is

the place of the full restitution of justice and originary beatitude.

4.8. Let us reflect on the correspondence that Dante establishes between the earthly paradise and the golden age whose return Virgil had announced. This implies that the earthly paradise was not, for Dante, a reality that is past and, as such, unattainable, but something that is in some way now happening or to come. It seems that Dante actually takes seriously the Virgilian prophecy of a return of originary justice on earth and that what he experiences in the divine forest is the realization of that prophecy. This realization is accompanied by another prophecy, the subject of which is the poet itself.

In Canti 29–32, Dante in fact arranges in the earthly paradise a prophetic experience that he himself compares without false humility to that of Ezekiel and that of John— namely, to the two highest points of visionary prophecy, respectively, of Judaism (the mysticism of the Merkavah or chariot) and of Christianity (John's Apocalypse):

> but read Ezekiel, who depicts them as he saw them
> come from the cold parts with wind and cloud and
> fire, and as you shall find them on his pages such

were they here, except that for the wings John is
with me and departs from him.

(ma leggi Ezechiel, che li dipigne
come li vide da la fredda parte
venir con vento e con nube e con igne;
e quali i troverai nelle sue carte
tali eran quivi, salvo ch' a le penne
Giovanni è meco e da lui si diparte.)

(Purgatorio 29.100–05)

To gauge the audacity of this visionary claim, with which
Dante puts himself on the same level as the greatest
prophets of the biblical tradition, it is necessary to remember that the vision of the chariot was so important in
Judaism that it could be an object of study only on the part
of the initiated (the *Ma' aseh Merkavah*, reads the Talmud,
'must not be explained even to one person alone, unless it
is a sage who understands it himself'). This prohibition was
also known to the Christian tradition, because Jerome, in
a letter that Dante could have been familiar with, recalls
that the rabbinic tradition prohibited the study of the Book
of Ezekiel to anyone who had not reached the age of 30
(which is the age that Dante has already reached at the
moment of his vision and also exactly the age the prophet

declares that he is at the moment in which 'the heavens were opened' for him). In his *Homilies on Ezekiel*—another text that Dante could have been familiar with—Gregory the Great observes that if Ezekiel declares that he had his vision *in tricesimo anno*, that is because only at 'that perfect age' (*in aetate perfecta*) can one receive the 'spirit of prophecy' (*Homeliae in Ezechielem* 2.3). And that what is in question for the poet is a prophetic experience is confirmed by the evocation of Ezekiel in the letter to Cangrande: *Et in Ezechiele scribitur: 'Vidi et cecidi in faciem meam'* ('And in Ezekiel it is written: "I saw and fell on my face"'). The poet, whose memory cannot fully cope with the vision, prophesies exactly as Ezekiel does at Chebar (the analogy is all the stronger since he was, like Dante, an exile who addressed himself to a people in exile).

Against the common interpretations that reduce it to a fanciful illustration of obvious truths contained in theological dogmas (the 24 elders are the books of Scripture, the animals are the evangelists, the griffin is Christ, the four women the cardinal virtues, etc.), it is important not to forget the prophetic and not merely descriptive character that Dante claims for his vision. Whatever interpretation that one could give of this—a problem on which we do not here intend to pronounce an opinion—the earthly paradise is the place that the poet chooses to announce a theological and political message that is certainly not orthodox, which could not be said otherwise than through a prophetic vision.

4.9. The vision, which fuses together elements drawn from the vision of Ezekiel and that of John, begins with the seven gold candelabras and with the 'twenty-four elders' from the Apocalypse (*vidi septem candelabra aurea* [Revelation 1:12]; *super thronos viginti quattuor seniores sedentes circumamictos vestimentis albis et super capita eorum coronas aureas* [Revelation 4:4]); immediately after he evokes the *quattuor animalia plena oculis ante et retro* (four living creatures covered with eyes before and behind) of Revelation 4:6, which derive from the four *Chayyot*, the 'animate creatures' of Ezekiel, from whom Dante also draws the image of the chariot, to which he adds, however, a griffin that is as unheard-of as it is enigmatic: 'The space between these four contained a tri-umphal chariot on two wheels, which came drawn at the neck of a griffin' (*Lo spazio dentro a lor quattro contenne / un carro, in su due ruote, triunfale, / ch' al collo di un grifon tirato venne*) (*Purgatorio* 29.106–08). What is inexplicably lacking in Dante's vision is precisely what constituted the centre of Ezekiel and John's prophetic visions, namely, the throne:

Statim fui in spiritu et ecce sedis posita erat in caelo et supra sedem sedens et qui sedebat similis erat aspectui lapidis ias- pidis et sardini et iris erat in circuitu sedis similis visioni zmaragdinae. ('At once I was in the spirit, and behold, there was a throne standing in heaven and on the throne there was one sitting, and the one who sat was similar in aspect to lapis lazuli and cornelian, and there was a rainbow around the throne similar to the vision of an emerald.') (Revelation 4:2)

Et super firmamentum quod erat inminens capiti eorum quasi aspectus lapidis sapphyri similitudo throni et super similitudinem throni similitudo quasi aspectus hominis desuper. ('And above the firmament that was over their heads there was something like a throne, in appearance like sapphire, and above the likeness of a throne was something that seemed like a man.') (Ezekiel 1:26)

This means that the object of the vision is not the glory of Christ ('this vision is a similitude of the glory of the Lord'; *Haec visio similitudinis gloriae Domini* [Ezekiel 2:1]) as common interpretations seem to suggest, but something else. The central personage, who occupies the place that in the two prophets concerned the figure on the throne, is in fact

Beatrice. As has been noted, the apparition of Beatrice is, like that of Matelda, described in unequivocally amorous terms ('I felt old love's great power. The lofty virtue smote on my sight which had already pieced me'; *d'antico amor sentì la gran potenza. / Tosto che ne la vista mi percosse / l'alta virtù, che già m'avea trafitto* [*Purgatorio* 30.39–41]; 'I know the marks of the ancient flame'; *conosco i segni de l'antica fiamma* [ibid. 30.48]). This is all the more the case in that, as has been observed, Beatrice herself evokes the title of Dante's first collection: 'these were such in his *new life* virtually, that every right habit would have come to marvellous proof in him' (*questi fu tal ne la sua vita nova / virtualmente, ch'ogni abito destro / fatto averebbe in lui mirabil prova*) (ibid. 30.115–17), where 'habit' is to be understood, as in *Convivio* 3.13.8, also in the technical sense of poetic and philosophical capacity, and the 'new life' is not only youth, but also and rather the amorous experience so effectively described in the prosimetrum. Without prejudice to other interpretations, it is obvious that, like Matelda, who is so intimately linked to her, Beatrice has to do with the amorous beatitude that, according to *De Monarchia* 3.15, constitutes the 'ultimate end' of human nature.

א. If the griffin were, according to the dominant interpretation, only a figure of the two natures of Christ, one would still need to explain why Dante removes it from the throne in which it sat in Ezekiel and in John and compels it to the carry out the task, certainly less glorious, of drawing the angelic chariot (while it should rather be the contrary). Nor can one understand why the poet must expressly underline a theological commonplace, namely Christ's two natures, divine and human. The two natures of the griffin could instead be those in which man participates according to *De Monarchia* 3.15.5:

> *Si ergo homo medium quoddam est corruptibilium et incorruptubil-ium, cum omne medium sapiat naturam extremorum, necesse est hominem sapere utramque naturam.* (If man holds a middle place between the corruptible and the incorruptible, then as every mean knows the nature of the extremes, it is necessary for man to know both natures.)

In this sense, Odo of Tournai had already defined man as one person in two substances, with respect to the creator who has multiple persons in one sole substance:

> The human person [. . .] consists of soul and body [. . .].
> The soul assumes the body in its person, with the result that there is a double substance in one person. This distinguishes the creature especially from the Creator, because the Creator has several persons in one substance, which utterly cannot be found in the creature. The creature is discovered to have one person in several substances (1984: 62–3).

As suggested by the passage already cited from *De Monarchia*, which follows immediately, the griffin would then be a symbol of upright human nature:

> *Cum omnis natura ad ultimum quendam finem ordinetur, consequitur ut hominis duplex finis existat* [. . .] *beatitudinem scilicet huius vite, que in operatione proprie virtutis consistit et per terrestrem paradisum figuratur; et beatitudinem vite eterne* [. . .] *que per paradisum celestem intelligi datur.* (And inasmuch as every nature is ordained for a certain ultimate end, it follows that there exists for man a twofold end [. . .] the beatitude of this life, which consists in the operation of his own virtue and is prefigured by the earthly Paradise; and the beatitude of life everlasting [. . .] which may be understood by means of the celestial Paradise.)

This would have the not-indifferent advantage of restoring to Dante's vision the political meaning, which is so forcefully present in Ezekiel and John that it would be problematic if it were missing precisely in Dante.

4.10. Our aim has not been that of furnishing an exhaustive interpretation of Canti 28–31 of the *Purgatorio*, but, more modestly, of situating Dante's conception of the earthly paradise with respect to the tradition of theological exegesis, showing not only its originality and novelty, but also its genuinely prophetic claim.

If the *subiectum* of the *Comedy* is, according to the letter to Cangrande, *homo prout merendo et demerendo per arbitrii libertatem iustitie premiandi et puniendi obnoxius est* ('man according as by his meriting or demeriting through his free will he is deserving or reward or punishment by justice') (*Letters* 10.11), then the earthly paradise is the place of a prophecy that could not fail to concern in some way the theme of the entire work: human freedom. It will be necessary, in fact, to restore its full weight to the explicit reference to the *Comedy* that Dante introduces into the first book of his political treatise (*De Monarchia* 1.12.6), connecting, significantly, the meaning of the two works: the *sicut in Paradiso Comedie iam dixit* ('as I have said in the *Paradiso* of the *Comedy*') referring to that 'greatest gift extended by God to human nature' which is freedom, 'through [which] we are happy here as men and elsewhere we will be happy through it as gods', does not refer only to Beatrice's affirmation in *Paradiso* 5.22 but also to the earthly paradise as eminent cipher of that liberty (Dante many times calls it simply 'paradise'—cf. *Paradiso* 7.38; *De vulgari eloquentia* 1.4.2; 1.5.3). The 'divine forest thick and lively' is thus for Dante a prophecy that concerns the possible salvation of man *per arbitrii libertatem*, up to the achievement here and now of that beatitude that consists 'in the use of the most beloved thing'.

ℵ. The doctrine of the earthly paradise as figure of the *beatitudo huius vitae* ('beatitude of this life') contradicts point-by-point the scholastic thesis, confirmed many times by Aquinas, according to which happiness is not possible for man in this life (*Impossibile est igitur in hac vita hominem totaliter esse felicem*) (*Summa Contra Gentiles* 3.48.7). Not only is there lacking in Aquinas Dante's distinction between earthly and heavenly beatitude, affirmed unreservedly in *De Monarchia*, but so also does the doctrine that Dante espouses in the *Convivio* 3.15.6 on the connection between knowledge and beatitude seem to be intentionally counterposed to Aquinas's thought, according to which 'man does not attain felicity, understood as his proper end (*prout est finis proprius eius*), during this life' (*Summa contra Gentiles* 3.48.11). Against those who doubt that 'wisdom is able to make a man happy without its being able to reveal certain things to him perfectly (namely, God, eternity, and primal matter)' (*Convivio* 3.15.7), so that his desire to know remains necessarily unsatisfying, Dante objects that

the natural desire within all things is proportionate to the capacity within that thing which has desire; otherwise desire would run counter to itself, which is impossible, and nature would have made it in vain, which is likewise impossible. It would run counter to itself because by desiring its perfection it would desire its imperfection, since it would always desire to continue desiring and would never fulfil its desire (and it is into this error that the accursed miser falls, by failing to perceive that he desires to continue desiring by seeking to realize an impossible gain) (ibid. 3.15.8).

It is likely that the one who doubts that knowledge can make man happy is here precisely Aquinas, who makes use of the *nummularii* (money changers), who 'insist on accumulating and multiplying money without limit' (*ad conservandum et multiplicandum denarios in infinitum*), to prove that human desire, insofar as it proceeds to the infinite, cannot be satisfied in this life: 'Because human desire proceeds to the infinite, they desire to the infinite the things with which they can satisfy their desire' (*Commentary on Aristotle's 'Politics'*, 1.8.4).

✿

5

Paradise and Human Nature

5.1. The earthly paradise—as we have seen—is the place where theologians pose the problem of human nature. And this happens by capturing human nature in an apparatus that condemns every attempt to define it to a split. This split is that between nature and grace. We are not dealing with a simple opposition: the two terms in reality form a system, within which they presuppose one another and constantly refer to each other in a relationship of inseparable division.

What is in question is, above all, the state in which Adam was created and the condition in which he found himself in paradise before sin. According to one opinion, which found its authoritative formulation in Peter Lombard,

Adam was created outside the Garden and placed in it only in a second moment, to signify that he was allowed to dwell there 'not by nature, but by grace':

> As scripture teaches, God took the man thus formed and placed him in the paradise of pleasure, which he had planted in the beginning. With these words, Moses openly says that man, created outside paradise (*extra paradisum creatus*), was subsequently placed in paradise (*postmodum in paradiso positus*). And it happened in this way because he was not to remain in it, or because it had been assigned to him not by nature, but by grace (*non ut naturae, sed gratiae*) (*Liber quattuor sententiarum* 1, dist. 17, ch. 5).

To these two moments of Adam's position outside and inside the earthly paradise there correspond two stages in the perfection of his nature: man was created first *in naturalibus*, and only in a second moment of time did he receive the *gratuita*, the gifts of grace. As Bonaventure writes, in reference to the discussions that divided the fathers on this problem:

> The most common and most likely opinion is that Adam received natural gifts (*naturalia*) before receiving those of grace (*gratuita*) [. . .]. According

to this opinion, it is therefore necessary to distinguish two moments in the state of innocence: the first, in which Adam had only natural gifts, and the second in which he also received the gifts of grace. If one accounts for the difference between these two moments, the apparent contradiction between the authorities of the fathers disappears (*In secundum librum Sententiarum* dist. 29, art. 2, q. 2).

In the same sense, Alexander of Hales had written:

It is fitting to the majesty of God that man be first created according to nature (*conditus secundum naturam*) and then informed through grace (*informatus per gratiam*), in a way that may recognize that grace is a gift of God and that it is thus distinct from natural gifts (*a naturalibus*) (*Summa universae theologiae* 1a–2ae, inq. 4, tract. 3, q. 3, t. 1, c. 1).

And yet, in the absence of any clear indication from the biblical sources, it is precisely the definition of what, in the originary condition, belongs to pure nature and what is instead reserved for grace that gave rise to proclamations so vague and, at the same time, peremptory that one has the impression that the distinction must be at all costs punctiliously maintained, even where it becomes impossible to do so.

5.2. That what is decisive in every case for the theologians is that nature and grace, while remaining indefinite, should be at once tightly interwoven and clearly divided in man, is obvious precisely in the author who, against the prior tradition, maintained that Adam was not created *in naturalibus*, but *in gratuitis*: Aquinas. In the *Summa Theologica* (1a, q. 95, a. 1, co.), he begins by citing the opinion of those who 'say that man was not created in grace; but that it was bestowed on him subsequently before sin', in order to immediately correct it. The justice (*rectitudo*) of the original state demands, in fact, that Adam was created in grace and not only in nature.

> For this rectitude [of the originary state] consisted in his reason being subject to God, the lower powers to reason, and the body to the soul: and the first subjection was the cause of both the second and the third; since while reason was subject to God, the lower powers remained subject to reason. Now it is clear that such a subjection of the body to the soul and of the lower powers to reason, was not from nature; otherwise it would have remained after sin; since even in the demons the natural gifts remained after sin. [. . .] Hence it is clear that also the primitive subjection by virtue

of which reason was subject to God, was not merely according to nature, but a supernatural gift of grace [. . .]. Hence if the loss of grace dissolved the obedience of the flesh to the soul, this means that the inferior powers were subjected to the soul solely through grace existing therein.

Natural justice, which belongs to man from the very beginning, is not, therefore, a natural good, but a *supernaturale donum*, a certain gratuitous gift given to the first man. And yet it has been granted not 'only to his person, but to the whole human nature that derives from him', at least as long as his will had not transgressed the divine precept (*De malo*, q. 4, a. 1, co.).

If already in these passages the difference between nature and grace is defined solely by means of sin, in such a way that nature is what remains when grace is taken away, in the other texts in which Aquinas investigates the question, the boundary that separates them becomes ever more subtle. Thus one reads in the commentary on Peter Lombard's *Sentences*:

All that which is directed to a certain end must be disposed as a function of the necessity of reaching it. But the end to which man is ordained—beatitude through the vision of God—is beyond the capacity of human nature [. . .]. It was thus necessary that human nature be constituted (*instituti*) in such a way that it should dispose not only of what belongs to it in virtue of its natural principles, but also something more (*aliquid ultra*), in virtue of which it could easily reach its end [. . .]. For this reason it was necessary, so that the more elevated part of the soul could turn freely towards God, that the inferior powers be submitted to it, in such a way that nothing in them could hold back the mind in its journey toward God. For the same motive, it was also necessary that the body be disposed in such a way that no passion should be produced that could impede the mind's contemplation. And since all this was in man in view of his end and sin had diverted him from it, it follows that all these goods ceased to exist in human nature and man was left (*relictus*) with his natural goods (*Super Sententiis* 2, d. 30, q. 1, a. 1, co.).

In this description, which would have pleased Pelagius, grace seems to penetrate so intimately into human nature to dispose it to its end ('It was thus necessary that human nature be constituted [. . .] it was also necessary that the body be disposed [. . .]') that it is impossible distinguish the natural gifts from it. Human nature was not simply created, but—with a term that belongs originarily to the lexicon of law—it was 'instituted' by grace. The distinction is, however, firmly maintained. Once again, in fact, the *naturalia* as such come to light—albeit negatively—when grace is taken away as a consequence of sin. This is so much the case that these natural goods, which are never clearly defined, figure both as inherent limits to the natural condition and, once grace is taken away, as punishments:

> If one considers human nature according to its natural principles, there is no doubt that they are not penalties, but simply natural defects (*defectus naturales*), like the fact of having been drawn from nothing and of having need to be maintained in being: these natural defects are common to all creatures and do not constitute a penalty for any of them. But if one considers human nature insofar as it was instituted, there is no doubt that they are penalties, because one says that someone has been punished when one has deprived him of something that had earlier been granted him (ibid.).

The residual and negative character of human nature is so essential to it that it can paradoxically appear as a punishment that man receives for having sinned, that is, for having lost grace. In any case, even before being split into *natura integra* and *natura lapsa*, human nature is divided between pure nature and grace. Human nature is what remains if it is separated from grace.

5.3. That human nature as such can come to light only if grace has been taken away from it is implicit in the comparison, to which theologians always make recourse, of grace to a garment. Before sin Adam and Eve did not notice their nudity, not through innocence, but because it was covered by a garment of grace. It is for this reason that Thomas de Vio (better known as Caietanus or Cajetan, the theologian whom the Church opposed to Luther in 1518), in his *Commentaries* on the *Summa Theologica*, can explain the difference between the 'pure' human nature and the originarily graced nature by comparing it to that which lies between a naked person and a person who has been stripped naked (*expoliata*). Just as the simple nudity of a body is different from that of the same body that has been stripped of its clothes, so too is human nature, which has lost that which was not nature (grace), different from how it was before grace had been added to it. Nature is now defined by the non-nature that it has lost, just as the body that has been made nude is defined by the clothes of which it has been stripped. Nature and grace, nudity and clothes together constitute a singular apparatus, whose elements seem autonomous and separable and yet, at least insofar as it concerns nature, do not remain unchanged after their separation. This means that nature—exactly like simple nudity—is, in reality, inaccessible: there is only its being made nude, only corrupt nature exists.

5.4. It has been aptly observed (Torrell 2008: 112) that, since Aquinas is convinced that man was created in grace, the hypothesis of a pure nature in Adam before sin is merely theoretical ('since it would have been possible,' he writes at a certain point, 'for God to create man *in puris naturalibus*, it is useful to consider to what point natural love could have extended' [*Quodlibet* 1, q. 4, a. 3, co.]). And yet the hypothesis must always be reaffirmed point by point, because in it what is at stake is the functioning of the apparatus through which human nature is defined. Even if Aquinas never speaks of a *natura pura*, he nevertheless many times (32, to be precise) makes use of the equivalent expression *pura naturalia* (pure natural things), to contrast these latter to the gifts of grace (*gratuita*), thanks to which alone man can progress towards the good (*non habet hoc ex* *naturalibus sed ex gratuitis* [*Super Sententiis* 2, d. 29, q. 1, a. 2, ad. 1]), because what is nature in man cannot count as merit for happiness (*illa quae sunt naturalia, non sunt meritoria* [ibid. 3, d. 30, q. 1, a. 4, ad. 1]).

What these purely natural goods could be is, even if not defined, at least suggested at the moment when he distinguishes the 'integral nature' of Adam in the state of innocence from that corrupted by the effect of sin. It is appropriate to linger on this passage, in which it is possible to glimpse the idea the theologians made for themselves of human nature, independently of the gifts of grace that God infused into it.

> In the state of integral nature (*in statu naturae integrae*), man's operative potential could wish and do by means of his natural gifts (*per sua naturalia*) the good proportionate to his nature, such as the good of acquired virtue; but not the good that exceeded his nature, such as the good of infused virtue. But in the state of corrupt nature (*in statu naturae corruptae*), man can never do that of which his nature was capable, so that he is unable to achieve by his own natural powers the good proportionate to it (*Summa Theologica* 1a–2a, q. 109, a. 2, resp.).

It is at this point that Aquinas attempts for the first time to define the *pura naturalia* that define the proper operation of the human being as we know it:

> Yet because human nature is not altogether cor-rupted by sin, so as to be completely deprived of natural good, even in the state of corrupted nature it can, by virtue of its natural endowments, work some particular good, such as to build dwellings, plant vineyards, and the like (*sicut aedificare domos, plantare vineas et alia huiusmodi*); yet it cannot do all the good natural to it, so as to fall short in nothing; just as a sick man can of himself make some movements, yet he cannot be perfectly moved with the movements of one in health, unless by the help of medicine he be cured (ibid.).

The brief summary of the *naturalia* derives from the *Hypognosticon*, a pseudo-Augustinian text in which the author, after having affirmed that free will is not sufficient with respect to things divine, enumerated in this way the goods that belong by nature to man:

> [Free will] causes him to want the goods that come forth from nature, like cultivating fields, eating, drinking, having friends, wearing clothes, building

houses, taking wives, raising livestock, and learning the arts of earthly things—in a word, to want the good that concerns the present life (*Hypognosticon* 3.4.5; *Patrologia Latina* 45.1623).

It is easy to recognize in this list the sphere of that 'operation of one's own virtue' in which Dante made the beatitude of this life to consist: not only elementary needs (eating, drinking, wearing clothes) but also the acts and techniques of social and family life (having friends, taking wives, the learning of arts). And it is this whole eminently human and earthly sphere, which persists and comes fully to light after the loss of grace, that sin marks with its corruption, rendering it insufficient with respect to its own ends.

5.5. It is possible, at this point, to try to describe the function of the apparatus in which the definition of human nature is in question according to Aquinas. Human nature is split into two elements, the *pura naturalia* and the *gratuita*, which appear in their proper identity only through an operator that enacts their separation once and for all and renders them intelligible as such. This operator is sin. And this holds both for pure nature, which is defined residually as what persists after grace has been taken away, and for grace, whose non-natural character is attested only in its disappearance through the effect of sin (the subjection of the soul to the body, in which it consists, 'was not from nature; otherwise it would have remained after sin'). What is natural is what remains when grace is taken away and grace is what disappears when the *naturalia* appear (when man 'was left [*relictus*] with his natural goods'). Nature is the remainder and, at the same time, the presupposition of grace (*gratuita praesuopponunt naturalia* [*De veritate* q. 27, a. 6, ad. 3]), and yet it is constitutively incapable of reaching its true end; grace is the *aliquid ultra*, the complement that must be added to nature to complete it (*gratia non tollit naturam, sed perficit* [*Summa Theologica* 1a, q. 1, a. 8, ad. 2]) and yet—except, in part, for the six hours of integral nature in paradise before sin—it cannot render it perfect in this life.

In any case, if the decisive factor of the apparatus is sin, one can then say that the true sense of the doctrine of original sin is that of splitting human nature and of impeding nature and grace from ever being able to coincide in it in this life. As is obvious in the title of Augustine's anti-Pelagian treatise, 'nature' *and* 'grace' are only the two fragments that result from the caesura worked out by the Adamic transgression.

5.6. The insufficiency of human nature implicit in the split between *naturalia* and *gratuita* comes to light in the doctrine of Adam's animal body in paradise. The incorruptibility and immortality of Adam's paradisiacal members before sin do not actually come from nature but from grace. Like the other living beings, he was created in an animal body, to which a gift of grace was added and which would remain such for the entire time of his sojourn in the Garden. 'Paradise,' writes Aquinas,

> was a fitting place for human habitation as regards the incorruptibility of the original state. Now this incorruptibility did not belong to man by nature, but by a supernatural gift of God (*non erat hominis secundum naturam, sed ex supernaturali Dei dono*). In order that this gift might be attributed to the grace God, and not to human nature, God made man outside of paradise, and afterwards placed him there, so that he might inhabit it in the time of his animal life (*ut habitaret ibi toto tempore animalis vitae*) and later be transferred into heaven, once he had attained the spiritual life (*Summa Theologica* 1a, q. 102, a. 4, co.).

Against those who affirmed that Adam had no need to nourish himself, because this would have implied a shameful emission of excrement, which was not in keeping with the dignity of the paradisiacal state, the functions of animal life—including digestion and defecation—are maintained (save, for this latter, to suggest that God had taken steps to eliminate its indecency: *fuisset divinitus provisum ut nulla ex hoc indecentia esset* [ibid. 1a, q. 97, a. 3, ad. 4]); but insofar as there is added to them every time something gratuitous, the sphere of what they are capable of without grace is devalued and reduced point by point. Adam's body is all the more articulated by a series of caesurae, which emphasize its defective animal character, the more the presence in it of a supernatural gift is asserted.

> For his (Adam's) body was incorruptible not by reason of any intrinsic vigour of immortality; rather there inhered in the soul a force given by God in a supernatural way (*vis quaedam supernaturaliter divinitus data*), whereby it was enabled to preserve the body from all corruption so long as it remained itself subject to God [. . .]. Since the rational soul exceeds the proportion of corporeal matter, it was fitting to give it at the beginning a virtue, by means of which it could preserve the body a manner surpassing the capacity of corporeal matter (ibid. 1a, q. 97, a. 1, co.).

5.7. Once again, the archetype of this doctrine of Adam's animal body is in Augustine. In *De civitate Dei*, he affirms unreservedly the animal and not spiritual character of the paradisiacal body:

> The first earthly man, drawn from the earth, was created in a living soul and not in a life-giving spirit, because this was reserved to him as a reward for his obedience. And therefore his body, which required food and drink to satisfy hunger and thirst, and which had not absolute and indestructible immortality, but by means of the tree of life warded off the necessity of dying and was thus maintained in the flower of youth—this body was doubtless animate but not spiritual; and yet it would not have been subject to death if, by sinning, it had not incurred the judgment that God had preannounced and threatened (13.23.1).

Augustine interprets the passage from 1 Corinthians 15:42–6 on the spiritual body of the resurrection in the sense that Paul intended to oppose to it the purely animal body in which Adam was created:

> According to the Apostle, the first man was created in an animal body. He wanted to distinguish the animal body, which we have now, from the

spiritual, which we will have in the resurrection, saying, 'It is sown in corruption, it is raised in incorruption; it is sown in dishonour, it is raised in glory; [. . .] it is sown an animal body, it is raised a spiritual body.' [. . .] And to show what an animate body is, he adds, 'Thus it was written, The first man, Adam, became a living soul.' In this he wanted to show what the animate body is, though with regard to the first man, who he was called Adam when he was created and the soul was infused in him by God, holy Scripture does not say, 'Man was made in an animal body,' but 'Man became a living soul.' By these words, the Apostle wants man's animal body to be understood. [. . .] And here he has revealed more explicitly that he was referring to the animal body when he wrote, 'The first man became a living soul' and to the spiritual with the words, 'The Last Adam became a life-giving spirit.' The animal body is the first, which is what the first Adam had, although it would not have been mortal if he had not sinned. It is the same one that we now also have, insofar as its nature has been changed and corrupted, because on sin there follows the necessity of death (*De civitate Dei* 13.23.2).

The dismissal of Adam's body on Augustine's part could not be more decisive, to such a point that he does not hesitate to force the interpretation of Genesis 2:7 ('The Lord blew into his nostrils a spirit of life and the man became a living soul') by suggesting without any foundation that holy Scripture (in reality, the Greek translation of the Septuagint) does not use for 'spirit' the term *penuma*, but *pnois*, 'a name more fitting to the creature than to the creator' (*De civitate Dei* 13.24.3). Adam's life in paradise is the life of an animal body.

5.8. What can Adam's body do in paradise without grace? What can a purely animal human body do? These questions define the theological status of human nature in its irremediable split. The more or less meticulous catalogue of the acts that man can achieve *in naturalibus* ('like cultivating fields, eating, drinking, having friends, wearing clothes, building houses, taking wives, raising livestock, and learning the arts of earthly things—in a word, to want the good that concerns the present life') coincides with the very scope of human beings' life on earth—and yet the theological apparatus separates them into a circumscribed and lacking sphere. And it does it not by taking away, but by adding something: grace, in such a way that, once this has been subtracted through sin, human life and actions are transformed into *pura naturalia*, marked by lacunas and defectiveness.

His very nature thus becomes insufficient for man. According to an adage attributed to Augustine and repeated infinite times by theologians, 'Adam could stand firm on his feet, but could not walk' (*Stare Adam poterat, pedem movere non poterat*, which Peter Lombard specifies in the sense that 'he was able not to decline from what he had received', but not to achieve the acts 'fit to merit him salvation' [*Liber quattuor sententiarum* 2, dist. 24, ch. 1]). The distinctions between 'animal body' and 'spiritual body' and between *naturalia* and *gratuita* do nothing but codify this insufficiency, just as that between *natura integra* and *natura corrupta* attests is irremediable permanence in human nature. The *natura integra* is something from which it suffices to subtract its clothing of grace for it to exhibit its faulty nudity, and sin is nothing but the operator of a defectiveness that was inscribed in it from the beginning. The earthly paradise, from which man, for this reason, could only be expelled, is not the cipher of human nature's perfection, so much as, instead, its constitutive lack.

The thought of Eriugena and Dante constitutes the most radical refutation of this doctrine. If God created man in the animal genus, this is, according to Eriugena, because he wanted to create in him nature in its entirety, in such a way that 'man is in all the animals and all the animals are in man'. There is only one 'vital motion' that pervades all living beings, each of which is in itself integrally life, because Aristotle's three vital potentials (vegetative, sensitive and intellective) are in reality one sole potential. Human nature, without need of the addition of grace, is 'entirely image of God in the animal and entirely animal in the image of God'. Sin, which is an act of will, can therefore never contaminate nature, which is in itself 'free and completely released from all sin', just as it is immune from all punishment, which concerns action and not nature.

These motifs, which with all likelihood were familiar to him, assume in Dante a markedly political tone. In the clear pronouncement of Marco Lombardo, what renders human beings culpable is 'bad leadership' and not nature (*non natura che in voi sia corrotta*). The objects of the meticulous and implacable penal edifice in the *Comedy* are human actions, and not nature, which was and again is, through Christ, innocent and free. Cohesively with these premises, the earthly paradise is the cipher of the *beatitudo huius vitae*, of the happiness individually and political possible on earth, and, by following his liberty and his sovereignty ('Free, upright and whole is your will / [. . .] / therefore over yourself I crown and miter you'; *libero, dritto e sano è tuo arbitrio /* [. . .] */ per ch'io te sovra te corono e mitrio* [*Purgatorio* 27.140–2]), man can, as Dante does, enter again into the Garden, in order to encounter there original innocence and original justice, personified in Matelda, the enamoured maiden who has never left it.

Dante's earthly paradise is the negation of the theologians' paradise, and it is at least strange that, despite this obvious and peremptory opposition, Dante continues to be interpreted through Aquinas and scholastic theology—confirmation, if we needed it, of the fact that nothing renders a work so obscure and illegible as its canonization.

✹

6

The Kingdom and the Garden

6.1. In his *Commentary* on Aquinas's treatise *De Deo effectore*, Francisco Suárez, while conceding that it was a question of 'a curious matter, which never was and never could be', asks at a certain point what would have been the condition of human beings if Adam had not sinned (*De statu quem habuissent in hoc mundo viatores, si primi parentes non peccarent*, reads the title of the fifth book). After having meticulously discussed the way in which human beings would have multiplied and reproduced in the state of innocence and condemned the opinion of those who maintain that there would have been bigamy, sterility and corporeal imperfections; after having examined the question of whether in the state of innocence virginity would be preserved even after matrimony and having enumerated 'the things of which human beings would make use in order to preserve their life', the theologian cannot fail to contend, in the chapter, with the problem of whether 'there would have been a political community, whether one thinks of villages, cities or kingdoms (*an essent in statu innocentiae propria communitas politica, sive pagi, sive civitates, sive regni*)' (*Commentary* 7.4).

That human beings born in the state of innocence would have been familiar with 'a domestic community (*societas domestica*), born of the union of husband and wife and the procreation of children' does not appear to him to be in doubt. By contrast, what seems more controversial to him is the necessity of the existence of a *societas politica*, since *in statu innocentiae* there would not have been enemies and every family would have been sufficient for its own needs. 'Yet,' he adds,

it seems that one must affirm that human beings, however long the state of innocence had endured, would have had among them a political society, as there can be in a perfect society or in a kingdom [. . .] the foundation of which is that the union of human beings in a state does not happen only by accident or through the corruption of nature, but is appropriate to human beings in any condition whatsoever and concerns their perfection (ibid. 7.6).

The image of this 'perfect society' that the theologian sketches in the pages that follow is very disappointing. To the question of whether there would be a 'dominion of man over man' (*dominium hominis ad hominem*), he responds by distinguishing a *dominium proprietatis*, which is that of master over slave, from a *dominium directivum seu gubernativum*, namely, of the capacity to command others and judge them in view of the common good (ibid., 7.11). While the first form of dominion has no reason to exist in the state of innocence, the second, which is familiar to us from the societies that we know, maintains its necessity even in the paradisiacal condition. Just as there would have been a power of governance of husband over wife, so also 'even in the state of a perfect community a dominion of jurisdiction (*dominium iurisdictionis*) would be necessary, which a prince has with respect to his subjects'. Suárez takes care to specify that this power of governance does not derive from sin, as some would suggest, but is inherent in the very nature of community (*non ex culpa sed ex ipsa rei natura sequitur*) and is in force 'in any condition of human nature whatsoever, whether pure, integral, or corrupted (*in omni statu naturae humanae, sive purae, sive integrae, sive lapsae)*'. The subjection corresponding to this dominion does not in any way decrease, according to Suárez, the perfection of the state of innocence, because it does not deprive human beings of their free will: 'That authority of governance therefore would not have been a compulsory power, through which the subjects are submitted to penalties, but ordained to lead to a greater good and the peace of the community.' Except that he specifies immediately that 'this is naturally understood for the subjects who persevere in their innocence: if it happened that any sinned, the situation would be different' (ibid. 7.12).

Aquinas himself had after all justified with even greater conviction the 'dominion of man over man' that is the duty 'of the one who has the power of governing and directing free men' (*Summa Theologica* 1a, q. 96, a. 4, co.). 'There are two reasons,' he writes,

> for which such a dominion of man over man would have been present in the state of innocence. The first is that man is naturally a social being, and so in the state of innocence he would have lived in a social way (*socialiter*). Now a social life cannot exist among a number of people if there is no one to direct it towards the common good;

for many, as such, seek many things, whereas one attends only to one. [. . .] The second is that if one man is superior to others in knowledge and justice, it would not be fitting that he did not make use of them for the benefit of others (ibid.).

6.2. Nothing so much as this description—fanciful and yet so lacking in imagination—of human society in a state of innocence proves that the earthly paradise does not in any way constitute a political paradigm for theologians. Its only significance in this sphere is exhausted with the exclusion of the dominion over slaves and of ownership of immovable goods (as for moveable goods and animals, Suárez takes care to specify that there will remain for them a *peculiare ius*), already affirmed many times by the ecclesiastical tradition independently of the paradisiacal condition. And yet an ancient tradition, which the theologians could not have been ignorant of, had put the earthly paradise in relation with the fundamental content of the gospel proclamation: the *basileia tou theou*, the Kingdom of God. This connection surfaces many times in the apocalyptic literature of late Judaism. In the prophetic vision that concludes the *Testament of Levi*, at the end of days, when the Lord 'will dwell in the midst of Israel', a new priest will arise, which will pronounce on the earth a 'judgment of truth' and will reopen to the just the doors of the earthly paradise:

> In this priesthood shall sin come to an end
> And the transgressors of the law will cease to do
> evil.
> And he shall open the gates of paradise,
> And shall remove the threatening sword against
> Adam.
> And he shall give to the saints to eat from the tree
> of life,
> And the spirit of holiness shall be on them.
>
> (18.9–11; Charles 2004: 314–15)

In the *Book of Enoch*, a text that had wide propagation in the early centuries of Christianity, the advent of the eschatological Kingdom coincided with the reappearance of the tree of life and the restoration of the paradisiacal condition. When Enoch asks what the fragrant tree that unexpectedly appears to him on a mountain top is, the angel responds:

> This high mountain which you have seen, whose summit is like the throne of God, is his throne, where the Holy Great one, the Lord of Glory, the Eternal King, will sit, when he shall come down

to visit the earth with goodness. And as for this fragrant tree no mortal is permitted to touch it till the great judgment, when he shall take vengeance on all and bring everything to its consummation forever. It shall then be given to the just and holy. Its fruit shall be food to the elect: it shall be transplanted to the holy place, to the temple of the Lord, the Eternal King. Then shall they rejoice with joy and be glad, and into the holy place shall they enter; and its fragrance shall be in their bones, and they shall live a long life on earth, such as your fathers lived, and in their days shall no sorrow or plague or torment or calamity touch them (25.3–6; Charles 2004: 204–05).

In the *Fourth Book of Ezra* as well, which until the Council of Trent was included in the text of the Vulgate, at the advent of the messiah, who will reign on earth for four hundred years, 'the furnace of Gehenna shall be made manifest, and over against it the paradise of delight' (7.36; Charles 2004: 583). In later Judaism, the earthly Kingdom, restored by the messiah from the line of David, culminates, after the defeat of the peoples that had oppressed Israel, in a banquet which takes place in the Garden of Eden, in the course of which the just will consume the flesh of Leviathan and Behemoth.

Certainly for the Christian tradition it is more significant that, of the three occurrences of the term 'paradise' in the New Testament, two are put in relation with the Kingdom. When the criminal crucified beside him says to him, 'Remember me when you enter into your Kingdom (*eis basileian sou*),' Jesus responds, 'Today you will be with me in paradise (*en tō paradeisō*)' (Luke 23:42), as if Kingdom and paradise were synonyms. And in Revelation 2:7, the Spirit announces that 'he will cause the victorious'— namely, those who, having overcome the eschatological test, can enter the eternal Kingdom—'to eat from the tree of life that is in the paradise of God'.

6.3. It is not surprising that, amid the silence of the theologians, religious movements often classified as heretical, up to that of the Free Spirit, which inspired Bosch's triptych at the Prado, had resolutely identified the earthly paradise with the Kingdom. Already among the early fathers, however, the relation between the Garden and the Kingdom is all the more present, the more it is conceived, following the tradition of Jewish apocalyptic, as an earthly kingdom that precedes the end of days. In John's Apocalypse, this kingdom in fact coincides with the thousand years in which Satan, 'the ancient serpent' (*ophis ho archaios*), is chained and thrown into the abyss:

> Then I saw an angel coming down from heaven, holding in his hand the key to the abyss and a great chain. He seized the dragon, that ancient serpent, who is the devil or Satan, and bound him for a thousand years, and threw him into the pit, and locked and sealed it over him, so that he would deceive the nations no more, until the thousand years were ended (Revelation 20:1–3).

At this point the 'first resurrection' (*hē anastasis hē protē*) occurs, after which those who have not worshipped the beast reign with Christ for a thousand years:

> Blessed and holy are those who share in the first resurrection. Over these the second death has no power, but they will be priests of God and of Christ, and they will reign with him for a thousand years (*basileusousin met' autou chilia etē*) (Revelation 20:6).

After Papias and Justin, who had accepted the apocalyptic tradition according to which the just after the resurrection of the body would reign happily on earth for a thousand years, it is in Irenaeus that one finds a true and proper theology of the thousand-year Kingdom developed. He refuses any allegorical interpretation of the passage from Revelation and of the other texts which he uses to prove the reality of the kingdom, from the Old Testament prophets (in particular Isaiah 11:6–10, Ezekiel 37:12–14 and Jeremiah 31:10–13) to Paul. 'All these things,' he writes, 'cannot be understood in reference to super-celestial realities [. . .] but to the times of the kingdom, when the earth will be renewed and Jerusalem will be reconstructed according to the model of the Jerusalem that is on high' (Irenaeus of Lyons 1969: 444).

The Kingdom has above all a cosmological meaning, whose chronology Irenaeus takes care to specify first of all. Picking up the indications of pseudo-Barnabas, he establishes a correspondence between the days of creation and the seven ages of the world:

> In the same number of millennia as of days in which the world was created, it is brought to completion. Thus says the holy book of Genesis: 'And the heaven and the earth and all their ornaments were brought to completion. And on the sixth day God brought to completion all the works that he had made and on the seventh day he rested from

all the works that he had made.' This text is not only a narration of past facts but also a prophecy of future events. If in fact 'a day for the Lord is like a thousand years' and in six days the things made were brought to completion, it is clear that six thousand years is their completion (ibid.: 358).

The seventh millennium corresponding to the seventh day is therefore the time of the kingdom, 'when the Lord will come from heaven on the clouds, drive the Antichrist and those who obeyed him into the lake of fire and give to the just the time of the kingdom, namely, rest' (ibid.: 386).

The theoretical nucleus of Irenaeus's doctrine, beyond the chronological identification of the Kingdom with the seventh millennium of world history, consists in the irre-nunciable demand for an earthly reality of redemption, insofar as in it what is immediately in question is the very originary status of creation. It is from the cosmological perspective of the Kingdom, in fact, that Irenaeus reads the passage from Romans 8:19–21 in which Paul had evoked 'the impatient waiting (*apokaradokia*) of nature which expects the revelation of the son of God'. If the apostle here pronounces that 'creation itself will be liber-ated from the slavery of corruption through the freedom of the glory of the son of God', this means that, together with all creation, in the thousand-year Kingdom human nature itself will be restored in its originary freedom and integrity: 'God is indeed rich in everything and all things belong to him. It is necessary then that the same natural condition be reintegrated into the origin to serve the just without any more prohibition (*et ipsam conditionem redintegratam ad pristinum sine prohibitione*)' (Irenaeus of Lyons 1969: 398).

The Kingdom is necessary, because human beings must find in their own earthly condition the happiness of which they have been deprived in it:

> It is just that they harvest the fruits of their suffering in the same condition in which they suffered and were put to the test in a thousand ways; that they be restored to life in the same condition in which they left it; that, finally, they reign in the same condition in which they bore slavery (*in qua conditione servitutem sustinuerunt, in ipsa regnare eos*) (ibid.).

In Irenaeus's theology of the Kingdom, temporal beatitude on earth must precede eternal beatitude, because in it what is at stake is the restoration of human nature to its original integrity.

It is not surprising, then, that at this point he explicitly evokes the earthly paradise. The dwelling of the just in the Kingdom can assume—he suggests—diverse forms and be located in heaven, in the restored Jerusalem, or in the earthly paradise: 'Some, held to have an affinity for dwelling in heaven, will ascend there, others will enjoy the delight of the Garden (*tēs tou paradeisou tryphēs apolausousin*), and others still the beauty and splendor of the city' (ibid.: 458). In any case, 'God will be seen everywhere', because 'all is of God, who gives to each the gift of the dwelling that is most fitting for him'.

6.4. 'Christ announced the Kingdom and the Church is what has come.' The problem that is hidden in this ironic saying of Alfred Loisy is so pressing that it has often seemed preferable simply to leave it aside. If the Kingdom is the essential content of the Gospel proclamation and if it is present in Christ beyond all doubt, then the question of the modalities of its reality with respect to the reality of the Church becomes decisive in every sense. This problematic knot comes to light in the fact that the theology of the Kingdom of Irenaeus and the early fathers is progressively eliminated in step with the strengthening of the institutional organization of the Church. It is significant that a century after Irenaeus's death, it was precisely the architect of the alliance between Empire and Church, Eusebius of Caesarea, who defined unreservedly the teachings of the early fathers on the Kingdom as a 'somewhat fantastic' doctrine (*mythikotera* [*Historia Ecclesiastica* 3.39.11]). Against this tradition, he reports the testimony of Christians who, when interrogated by Domitian, had affirmed that 'the Kingdom of Christ is not temporal and earthly, but heavenly and angelic and would appear at the end of the world, when he would come in glory to judge the living and the dead' (ibid. 3.20.4).

Particularly instructive is the case of Tertullian, in whose work it is possible to grasp the passage from the earthly conception of the kingdom to the heavenly and spiritual one. In his burning polemic with Marcion, who denied the salvation of the flesh, he seems to profess the apocalyptic faith in an earthly kingdom, 'situated in Jerusalem, which will be made to descend from heaven by a divine work' (*Adversus Marcionem* 3.24.3). He insists, however, on its spiritual character, defining its innermost nature as 'heavenly' (*Haec ratio regni celestis*, he writes with a formula that the embarrassed editors of the *Corpus Christianorum* have proposed to emend to *subcaelestis*). He is reporting the news, confirmed also by pagan witnesses, that 'in Judea for four days one saw hovering in the air in the morning hours a city, whose walls vanished with the advance of daylight', and he suggests, with a probable citation from Irenaeus, that it has been prepared by God 'to gather the saints who rise again [. . .] because it is worthy of God that his servants should exult precisely where they were afflicted in his name' (ibid.); but he takes care to specify that 'our citizenship (*politeuma nostrum sive municipatum*) is in heaven' (ibid.). It is not surprising, therefore, that in *On the Resurrection*, he resolutely critiques as Jewish the doctrine of the earthly Kingdom. The Jews, who 'expect only earthly things and lose the things of heaven', identify the holy land with the soil of Judea, while it is none other than 'the flesh of Christ in all those who have been clothed with Christ' (ibid. 26.10–11). The Jerusalem whose restoration Isaiah announces is not the city that killed the prophets and stoned those who had been sent to it. With a radicality that goes beyond the critique of Judaism, he affirms that 'salvation is promised to no land, because it is necessary that it perish with the figure of the entire world' (ibid. 26.13).

Once again, the negation of the earthly kingdom coincides with the exclusion of the restoration of the paradisiacal condition.

And this is so even if one dares to maintain that the holy land is instead paradise, which is also called the paradise of the progenitors, namely Adam and Eve, insofar as there has been promised to the flesh a reintegration in paradise, which had been entrusted to it to guard and cultivate it, so that man may be called there again in the condition in which he was expelled from it (ibid. 26.14).

6.5. In *City of God*, Augustine comments on the passage from Revelation (20:7–9) on the Kingdom of the just, in order to save it from any milleniaristic interpretation. While confessing that he had once believed in the millennium, he now unreservedly liquidates as a 'ridiculous fable' the idea of this 'holy holiday at the end of the six thousand years of labours (*vacatione scilicet sancta post labores annorum sex milium*)' (*City of God* 20.7.1). 'Such things,' he writes scornfully without naming the fathers in question, 'can be believed only by the carnal. The spiritual define those who profess them with the Greek word *chiliastai*, whom we can call millenarians (*miliarios*) in the same way' (ibid.). The thousand years of which John spoke are to be understood not as the last part of the six millennia of world history, so much as rather, with a sort of forced numerological game, as if they signified the very fullness of time (*ipsa temporis plenitudo*):

> He has certainly used the thousand years as an equivalent for the whole duration of this world, employing the number of perfection to mark the fullness of time. For a thousand is the cube of ten. For ten times ten makes a hundred, that is, the square on a plane. But to give this plane height, and make it solid, the hundred is again multiplied by ten, which gives a thousand [. . .] with how much greater reason is a thousand put for totality (*pro universitate ponuntur*), since it is the cube of the decimal square (ibid. 20.7.2).

Augustine's decisive performance is, however, the neutralization of what is said in John's passage in which one reads unequivocally that 'the just will reign with him (Christ) for a thousand years'. With a gesture that would have a long lineage in the history of the Church and in Christian historiography, he simply identifies the Kingdom with the time of the Church, the very one in which the just and the wicked live together up to the moment when they will be separated in the day of judgement. Augustine is aware that the word 'Kingdom' thus loses its proper meaning, but he suggests that it is precisely to be understood in a 'very different and unequal' sense (*alio aliquo modo, longe quidem impari*) with respect to the Kingdom that will be after the end of days. And it is in this minor sense that 'there reign with him now his saints, of whom he says: "Behold, I am with you always, even to the end of days," otherwise the Church could not be called already now his Kingdom or the Kingdom of heaven' (ibid. 20.9.1). Certainly, in this Kingdom are gathered both the wheat and the weeds, both those who observe the precepts and those who transgress them; and yet the Church is and remains the earthly kingdom of God.

> Even now the Church is the kingdom Christ and the kingdom of heaven. And there reign with him also now his saints, though in another and far different way than how they will reign then; and with him do not reign the tares, even if, in the Church, these grow together with the wheat (ibid.).

It has been justly observed that Augustine, by resolving in this way an eschatological event into a historical period, killed the expectation of the Kingdom (Nigg 1944: 144). Insofar as it coincides with the historical existence of the Church, the Kingdom is emptied of all political significance and identified with the earthly vicissitudes of the city of God, which lives together in intimate distance with the earthly city up to the end of days.

א. In neutralizing the Kingdom in this way, Augustine inaugurated, more or less consciously, the representation of a single historical time, which rendered possible the birth of the Christian historiography that was inspired by him, from Orosius's *Historiae adversus paganos* to Odo of Freising's *Historia de duabus civitatibus*. In this sense, Odo could consider himself to be faithful to Augustine, affirming, in the prologue to the fifth book of his *Historia*, that he has 'woven the history as if of one sole city, which I call Church' (*Videor mihi non de duabus civitatibus, sed pene de una tantum, quam ecclesia dico, historiam texuisse*). With the Augustinian neutralization of the thousand-year Kingdom, historiography eliminated from itself a deeply heterogeneous element, which would have introduced into chronology an irreducible rupture. The extent to which modern historians inherit from the medieval chroniclers precisely this homogeneous historical space is a problem that cannot be confronted here.

6.6. That the Kingdom is in the Gospels an existing reality which coincides with the presence, words, and actions of Jesus, is a fact that no theologian would feel themselves capable of denying. Not only does Jesus, to the one who asks, 'When will the kingdom come?', respond unequivocally that it has already arrived (Luke 11:20: *ara ephthasen* *eph' hymas hē basileia tou theou*; 'now has the Kingdom of God come to you'), but the presence of the Kingdom is always expressed with verbs in the perfect, which in Greek refers unequivocally to an event that is already completed (Mark 1:15: *peplerotai ho kairos kai ēggeiken hē basileia tou theou*; 'the time has been fulfilled and the Kingdom of God has been made near'—the adverb *eggys*, from which the verb *eggizō* comes, etymologically means 'to hand'). And it is by now established that Jesus's response to the Pharisees who ask him when the Kingdom will come, *entos hymōn estin* (Luke 17:21), does not mean 'it is within you', but 'in the midst of you' or, more precisely, 'at hand, in the sphere of possible action'.

Other passages, however, such as Matthew 25:31–4, seem to speak of the Kingdom as a future reality, which will happen when the Son of Man comes in his majesty and sits on his thrown of glory: 'Then the king will say to those who stand at his right: "Come, you who are blessed by my father, inherit the Kingdom prepared for you since the origin of the world."' The Kingdom is, here, a future event and, at the same time, something that has existed since the beginning of time. The same Gospel that announced the immediate presence of the Kingdom shifts it into a time to come: 'They will come from east and west, from north and south,

and they will sit at the banquet in the Kingdom of God'
(Luke 13:29). Hence the perplexity of theologians as to the
temporal status of the Kingdom as *eschaton*, as a last time:
over the supporters of 'realized eschatology', who affirm
that the texts that seem to hint at a future time are to be
interpreted with reference to present fulfilment, there pre-
dominate the dialectical or progressive interpretations,
according to which the presence of the Kingdom is broken
down into an 'already' and a 'not yet', with respect to
which the intermediate time is the time of salvation, which
has already begun but still awaits its final realization. Thus
the Kingdom loses its reality and is transformed into a kind
of transition phase in a process whose fulfilment tends to
be infinitely deferred.

א. If it is true, as Walter Benjamin suggests, that in the idea of a
classless society Karl Marx secularized the idea of the messianic
kingdom, it is not surprising that here there are produced the same
aporias and the same diatribes that divide theologians over the way
in which one should think the articulation of eschatological time.
The problem of the interminable duration of the transition phase
between prehistory and history, between the society divided into
classes and that without classes, on which the Soviet Revolution
made shipwreck, corresponds perfectly to the genuinely theological
one over the timing of the coming of the Kingdom. And to the

problem of the compatibility between the Church and the Kingdom there corresponds the equally aporetic one of the compatibility between the party and the classless society.

6.7. The term *parousia*, to indicate the full presence of Christ at the end of days, is a typically Pauline expression. In the Synoptics, it appears only in Matthew 24: to the disciple who asks him 'what will be the sign of the *parousia* [the Vulgate translates it as *adventus*] and of the end of days', Christ responds by comparing the *parousia* of the Son of Man to the lightning 'that comes from the east and shines in the west' and to the flood that 'carries everything away'. By making use of the formula 'in (or through) the *parousia* of the lord Jesus Christ' at least six times, Paul seems to break down the messianic event into two moments: the resurrection and the second coming of Christ at the end of days. The translation of *parousia* as 'coming' (*adventus*) is not correct, however: the term means in Greek simply 'presence' (*para-ousia*, literally 'being beside', as if, in the present, being were situated, so to speak, beside itself). It does not designate a second event, which is added to the first to complete it. Paul makes use of it to think the peculiar structure of the messianic event, composed of two heterogeneous times, a *kairos* in which all times are contracted into one (*ho kairos synestalmenos estin*; 'time has been contracted' [1 Corinthians 7:29]), and a *chronos*, in which time stretches out as if beside itself. What are in question are not, that is to say, two moments in a chronology, but a messianic transformation of time: it is a matter, in every case, of grasping a presence, but this is such as to entail a radical alteration of the experience of time, which prevents us from locating it merely in a deter-minate chronological point. The same can be said for the Kingdom: it is present here and now, but is, at the same time, always in the act of coming, always ad-venting (Italian: *ad-veniente*), without this being able to imply a deferral. The so-called 'delay of the *parousia*', of which modern theologians incautiously speak, is for Paul simply unthinkable. The Kingdom for him is not a period of time between two events—the resurrection and the *parousia*—which punctually delimit it. It is entirely complete ('God has rescued us from the dominion of darkness and trans-ferred us into his Son's Kingdom of love' [Colossians 1:13]), but cannot be inscribed into chronological time ('If you have died with Christ, why do you argue over opinions as if you lived in the world?' [Colossians 2:20]).

6.8. The problem Paul must contend with here is the same one which we must always confront when we seek to think a reality—the Kingdom, the messianic event—in its emergingness (Italian: *sorgività*), without being able to insert it, as historiography does, into a representation or a predetermined chronology. Benjamin has written in this connection that when one wants to grasp a phenomenon dialectically or monadologically outside of the *continuum* of the linear historical reckoning, it is polarized and split according to its pre-history and its post-history, which does not mean simply past and present but designates two immanent forces in the field of tensions into which the phenomenon has thus been transformed (Benjamin 1982: 587–8, 594). The object can now be seized in its unity only through this polarization.

We can say, then, that the earthly paradise and the Kingdom are the two partitions that result from theologians' attempts to think human nature and its possible beatitude. They are split into a pre-historic element (the Garden of Eden) and a post-historical element, the Kingdom, which nevertheless remain separate and out of communication and, as such, inaccessible. The steady polemic against the chiliasts, who tend to identify the earthly kingdom with the paradise of origins, has precisely this function. The Garden must be driven back into an archi-past, which it is no longer possible to obtain in any way; the Kingdom, when it is not simply flattened into the Church and in this way neutralized, is projected into the future and displaced into the heavens.

Against this forced separation of the two poles, we must remember, with the chiliasts and Dante, that the Garden and the Kingdom result from the split of one sole experience of the present and that in the present they can therefore be rejoined. The happiness of human beings on earth is stretched between these two polar extremes. And human nature is not a pre-existent and imperfect reality, which must be inscribed through grace into an economy of salvation, but it is what always appears here and now in the coincidence—that is, in the falling together—of paradise and Kingdom. Only the Kingdom gives access to the Garden, but only the Garden renders the Kingdom think-able. Or rather: we grasp human nature historically only through a politics, but this latter, in its turn, has no content other than paradise—which is to say, in Dante's words, 'the beatitude of this life'.

❀

Bibliography

The texts of Ambrose, Augustine and Aquinas are cited as is customary, indicating the books, chapters and paragraphs. The edition of Ambrose's *De paradiso* utilized is *Ambrosii Episcopi Mediolanensis Opera* (Carolus Schenkl ed.) (*Tutte le opere di sant'Ambrogio*, VOL. 2, PART 1, *Il paradiso terrestre. Caino e Abele. Noè* [Paolo Siniscalco ed.] [Rome: Città Nuova, 1984]). The anti-Pelagian works of Augustine are cited from the CSEL (*Corpus Scriptorum Ecclesiasticorum Latinorum*), VOLS 42, 44, 60. The edition of the *Periphyseon* (*Division of Nature*) is that edited by Nicola Gorilani: John Scotus Eriugena, *Della divisione della natura* (Milan: Bompiani, 2013), which reproduces the text of the critical edition of Édouard Jeauneau, in VOLS 161–5 of the *Corpus Christianorum: Continuatio Mediaevalis*.

Translator's Note: For all ancient and medieval sources, while I have at times consulted existing English translations, I have opted for a rendering as close as possible to Agamben's Italian—at times simply translating his Italian directly, in consultation with the original. This is especially the case for biblical citations, where Agamben is often comparing the Hebrew, Greek and Latin versions. Even when existing English translations have been cited, they have frequently been revised. Aside from the sources listed in Agamben's note above and in the bibliography below, Agamben also cites a variety of patristic and medieval texts that can be found in standard editions such as Migne's *Patrologia Latina* or the more contemporary *Corpus Christianorum* or *Sources chrétiennes* series.

AMBROSIASTER. 1966. *Ambrosiastri qui dicitur Commentarius in Epistulas Paulinas, Volume 1: In Epistulam ad Romanos* (Heinrich Joseph Vogels ed.). Vindobonae: Hoelder-Pichler-Tempsky (CSEL, 81/1). English translation: 2009. *Commentaries on Romans and 1– 2 Corinthians* (Gerald L. Bray ed. and trans.). Downers Grove, IL: Intervarsity Press.

ANSELM. 1990. *De conceptu virginali et de originali peccato* in *L'Œuvre de Anselme de Canterbury, Volume 4: La conception virginale et le péché originel. La procession du Saint Esprit. Lettres sur les sacrements de l'Église. Du pouvoir et de l'impuissance* (Michel Corbin ed.). Paris: Cerf. English translation: Anselm of Canterbury. 1998. *On the Virgin Conception and Original Sin* (Camilla McNab trans.) in *The Major Works* (Brian Davies and G. R. Evans eds). New York: Oxford University Press, pp. 357–89.

AQUINAS, Thomas. 1975. *Summa Contra Gentiles, Book 3: Providence, Part 1* (Vernon J. Bourke trans.). South Bend, IN: University of Notre Dame Press.

——. 2003. *On Evil* (Brian Davies ed., Richard Regan trans.). New York: Oxford University Press.

——. 2007. *Commentary on Aristotle's 'Politics'* (Richard J. Regan trans.). Indianapolis, IN: Hackett.

——. 2008[1920]. *The Summa Theologica of St. Thomas Aquinas*, 2nd revd ed. (Fathers of the English Dominican Province trans.). Available online at: http://www.newadvent.org/summa (last accessed on 29 February 2020).

AUGUSTINE. 1993. *The City of God* (Marcus Dods trans.). New York: Modern Library.

BENJAMIN, Walter. 1982. *Das Passagen-Werk* in *Gesammelte Schriften*, VOL. 5, PART 1. Frankfurt am Main: Suhrkamp.

BREMMER, Jan N. 2008. *Greek Religion and Culture: The Bible and the Ancient Near East*. Boston, MA: Brill.

BRAGA, Corin. 2004. *Le paradis interdit au Moyen-Âge*. Paris: Editions L'Harmattan.

CAVALCANTI. 2007. *Thirty-Six Selected Poems Including 'Donna me prega'* (A. S. Kline trans.). Available online at: http://bit.ly/3cfTkYR (last accessed on 29 February 2020).

CHARLES, R. H. (ed.). 2004. *The Apocrypha and Pseudepigrapha of the Old Testament, Volume 2: Pseudepigrapha*. Berkeley, CA: Apocryphile Press.

DANTE ALIGHIERI. 1904. *The De Monarchia of Dante Alighieri* (Aurelia Henry ed. and trans.). New York: Houghton, Miflin. Available online at: http://bit.ly/3ag6seI (last accessed on 29 February 2020).

———. 1920. *The Letters of Dante / Dantis Alagherii Epistolae* (Paget Toynbee ed. and trans.). New York: Oxford University Press.

———. 1939. *The Divine Comedy: Inferno, Purgatorio, Paradiso* (John D. Sinclair trans.). New York: Oxford University Press.

———. 1990. *Il Convivio (The Banquet)* (Richard H. Lansing trans.). Garland Library of Medieval Literature. Available online at: http://bit.ly/32C9t6w (last accessed on 29 February 2020).

FITZMEYER, Joseph A. 1993. 'The Consecutive Meaning of EΦ' Ω in Romans 5.12'. *New Testament Studies* 39: 321–39.

FRÄNGER, Wilhelm. 1951. *The Millennium of Hieronymus Bosch: Outlines of a New Interpretation* (Eithne Wilkins and Ernst Kaiser trans). Chicago: University of Chicago Press.

HAMMOND BAMMEL, Caroline P. 1985. *Der Römerbrieftext des Rufins und seine Origenes-Übersetzung*. Freiburg: Herder.

IRENAEUS OF LYONS. 1969. *Contre les hérésies*, VOL. 5, PART 2. Sources chrêtiennes, 153. Paris: Cerf.

JEROME. 1959. *Hebraicae quaestiones in libro Geneseos* in *S. Hieronymi presbyteri Opera, pt. 1, Opera exegetica, Volume 1: Hebraicae quaestiones in libro Geneseos. Liber interpretationis Hebraicorum nominum. Commentarioli in Psalmos. Commentarius in Ecclesiasten* (Paul de Lagarde, Germain Morin and Marc Adriaen eds). Corpus Christianorum. Series Latina, 72. Turnholti: Brepols.

NIGG, Walter. 1944. *Das ewige Reich: Geschichte einer Sehnsucht und einer Enttäuschung*. Zurich: Rentsch.

ODO OF TOURNAI. 1984. *On Original Sin, and A Disputation with the Jew, Leo, Concerning the Advent of Christ, the Son of God: Two*

Theological Treatises (Irven M. Resnick ed.). Philadelphia: University of Pennsylvania Press.

ORIGEN. 1992–93. *Commentarii in Epistulam ad Romanos. Römerbrief-Kommentar* (Theresia Heither ed.); *Volume 2: Liber tertius, Liber quartus*; *Volume 3: Liber quintus, Liber sextus*. Freiburg: Herder.

PASCOLI, Giovanni. 2002. *Poesie e prose scelte* (Cesare Garboli ed.). Milan: A. Mondadori.

SCHREINER, Thomas R. 2014. 'Original Sin and Original Death' in Hans Madueme and Michael Reeves (eds), *Adam, the Fall, and Original Sin: Theological, Biblical, and Scientific Perspectives*. Grand Rapids: Baker Academic, pp. 271–88.

SINGLETON, Charles. 1958. *Journey to Beatrice*. Cambridge, MA: Harvard University Press.

THEODORET OF CYRUS. 1998. *Commentario alla Lettera ai Romani* (Francesca Cocchini and Lella Scarampi eds). Rome: Borla.

TORRELL, Jean-Pierre. 2008. *Nouvelles recherches thomasiennes*. Paris: Vrin.

XENOPHON. 1914a. *Cyropaedia* in *Xenophon in Seven Volumes*, VOLS 5 and 6 (Walter Miller trans.). Cambridge, MA: Harvard University Press.

———. 1914b. *Oeconomicus* in *Xenophon in Seven Volumes*, VOL. 4 (Walter Miller trans.). Cambridge, MA: Harvard University Press.